6316

VALLEY OF DECISION

Sterling E. Lacy, Ph.D.

Dayspring Productions, Inc.
P.O. Box 7677
Texarkana, Texas 75505

VALLEY OF DECISION

— FORWARD —

Valley of Decision will take the reader on a fast-paced trip from the thoughts of our Founding Fathers to the thoughts of today's leaders. The ideas being projected today toward our youth, our families, and our country would literally have Washington, Franklin, Jefferson, Madison, and the others, spinning in their graves.

Dr. Lacy documents the Christian moorings of our nation and calls all men of goodwill to help restore them. He mentions some of the unmentionables, such as the Council on Foreign Relations and the Trilateral Commission. He records their beginnings, their power over modern America and what they are really up to. This in itself should cause you to stop, think, and act.

If you truly value freedom, if America means to you what it does to me, then *Valley of Decision* is a book for you.

Jim Jeffries
Member of Congress
(Ret.)
January 1988

* * * * *

Special thanks to
John F. McManus for editorial assistance
and Julie Hays for proofreading.

* * * * *

— TABLE OF CONTENTS —

PREFACE

TOPEKA, KANSAS, June 1978. *"Hello, Dr. Lacy. This is Alan Speck with ABC news in Washington. I understand you are getting ready to mass distribute another letter exposing a politician's vote on moral issues. Well, we are preparing a documentary on the Christian Right and we would like to come to Topeka to film your whole process and interview you."*

That's the first I had heard about the Christian Right. It sure was surprising to hear that I was part of something I had never heard of. Mr. Speck's call convinced me of two things. First, I must not be the only born-again Christian across America who was beginning to let his spiritual conviction guide him in the political arena. Second, I suspected that this documentary was an opening salvo against Christians everywhere who were doing the same.

It's partly our fault. About one hundred years ago the spiritual forefathers of today's born-again Christians resigned from the political arena and declared it unclean. Gallant patriots have fought America's gradual and almost complete slide into collectivism and amorality[1] with little or no help from America's Bible-believing Christians and sometimes with out-and-out opposition.

The purpose of this book is to explain to fellow Americans where Christians who make their voices heard in politics are coming from and where we are headed in the political arena. In fact, there's a good chance that a Bible-believing Christian made this book available to you so that you can accurately sort out our real position from the twisted portrayal of conservative Christians constantly offered by today's national media, the entertainment industry, and government education.

Conservative Christians believe that God created nationhood and has given guidelines for civil governments. We believe that America's forefathers wisely followed those guidelines and that's why America has experienced God's

---

1. Amorality is the position that there is no absolute God-given right or wrong.

blessings, one of which is the greatest amount of freedom any people have ever known.

We also believe that Americans are losing the battle for freedom over their own lives because they have allowed their nation to depart from God's guidelines. In fact, we believe that certain identifiable anti-God forces have successfully seized control of the direction America is heading and have led our beloved country to crawl into bed with the enslaving philosophies of the European nations from which our forefathers fled several centuries ago.

The terms "born-again Christian," "Bible-believing Christian" and "conservative Christian" will be used interchangeably to represent that body of Christianity that believes that there is a personal God, that Jesus is the Son of God and Lord of all, and that the Holy Spirit is not only sent to dwell in the child of God but has also inspired the writers of the Bible so that the Bible is not just a collection of man's ideas about God, but is God's revelation of His nature and His will for mankind.

The Bible speaks of a time when God will call all nations to a "valley of decision."[2] While none of us knows for sure when that final judgment will come, it is obvious that America needs to be called to her "valley of decision" now. There are two clear paths before us. One is the path of collectivism and amorality leading to world government and slavery at the hands of the declared enemies of God. The other is the path of individual responsibility, limited government and morality reflecting a commitment to God's principles and to freedom.

Valley of Decision calls America back to the crossroad faced by our forefathers two hundred years ago. It asks today's Americans for a fresh decision and a renewed commitment to travel the path that gives life and freedom under God's law.

It's our *Valley of Decision*, America. Let us choose wisely.

Sterling E. Lacy, Ph.D.
Texarkana, Texas
January, 1988

2. Joel 3:14 - Multitudes, multitudes in the valley of decision! For the day of the Lord is near in the valley of decision.

"The foundations of our society and our government rest so much on the teachings of the Bible that is would be difficult to support them if faith in these teachings would cease to be practically universal in our country."

— *Calvin Coolidge*

— 1 —
POLITICS AND RELIGION DON'T MIX

A pastor friend of mine was shocked recently upon returning from Washington where he had served as Chaplain of the House of Representatives for a day. He was shocked by the mail he had recently received from local persons condemning him for mixing politics and religion.

Politics is the science or art of civil government. At question here is whether or not God is interested in the science or art of civil government. If God is interested in civil government and civil governing, then the Bible-believing Christian will also be interested. If God is not, then that Christian will not be. It's as simple as that.

So, let's take a look at what the Bible says about God's interest in nations and civil government — politics, if you please.

One day while preaching to a pretty intellectual crowd in Athens, the apostle Paul (who was quite an intellectual himself) proclaimed it was God Himself who created the nations.[1] Moses claimed that this took place at the tower of Babel when God confused man's language,[2] which led to the scattering of mankind over all the earth. Since God is not a God of confusion,[3] it is not too surprising to find God interested in

1. Act 17:26 - "From one man he made every nation of men, that they should inhabit the whole earth; and he determined the times set for them and exact place where they should live."

2. Genesis 11:1-9.

3. I Corinthians 14:33.

establishing governing authorities to administer civil government. In fact, the Bible says that "there is no authority except that which God has established."[4] I don't believe for a minute that this means God hand-picked Hitler to rule Germany but rather that Hitler misused the God-given authority of civil government in his mad scheme to rule the world.

Civil authority is not an arena established by man when God wasn't watching. Nor is it a domain into which God rudely intruded when He decided man was not running things well. On the contrary, God created the entire basis for political administration and then man stomped in, ignored God's guidelines, and made a mess of things.

"But this is America," the modern critic cries out. "We pulled ourselves up by our own bootstraps. No God had anything to do with the founding of our government. I had twelve years of government education and four years at the university and there was never anything in any of my textbooks about some God or Bible molding our government at its beginning. You Twentieth-Century Christians are just trying to cram God down our throats and take over our government. Look for yourselves. Our government was created by the Constitution, the Declaration of Independence, and the likes of Benjamin Franklin, Patrick Henry and George Washington."

Indeed it was. But it's interesting to go back to the writings of those men themselves to see what role they thought God and the Bible played at the founding of the American government.

For instance, during one session of the Constitutional Convention when the delegates were hopelessly bogged down in dissension, aging Benjamin Franklin rose to say:

> I have lived, Sir, a long time, and the longer I live, the more convincing proofs I see of this truth: that God governs in the affairs of man. And if a sparrow cannot fall to the ground without His notice, is it probable that an empire can rise without His aid? We have been assured, Sir, in the Sacred Writings, that except the Lord build the house, they labor in vain that build it. I firmly believe this...

4. Romans 13:1.

I therefore beg leave to move that henceforth, prayers imploring the assistance of Heaven and its blessing on our deliberation be held in this assembly every morning.[5]

Not only was this done, but every assembly of our Congress in the entire history of our government has been opened with prayer to God.

The signers of the Declaration of Independence not only sealed their fates with their signatures on that great document, but they sealed the Declaration itself with an acknowledgement that they were dependent upon God for the success of their great venture. They stated: "For the support of this declaration, with a firm reliance on the protection of the Divine Providence, we mutually pledge to each other, our lives, our fortunes, and our sacred honor."[6]

As to Patrick Henry and George Washington, here is a sample of what they had to say about God and/or the Bible: "The Bible is worth all other books which have ever been printed" —Patrick Henry,[7] and, "It is impossible to rightly govern the world without God and the Bible" —George Washington.[8]

Similar quotes from other early American leaders would fill thousands of pages. Suffice it to say that these God-fearing men created the American government with God's principles foremost in mind.

We will take a look at those principles later, but let us now establish why it is important, even essential, for God's children to mix politics and religion. First, let us look at God's interest in politics.

God is interested in the political arena for several good reasons. God created everything seen and unseen, on earth and in heaven, including thrones, powers, rulers and authorities.[9]

5. Rus Walton, "Evidences of Our Christian Heritage," *The Rebirth of America* (Philadelphia, PA: The DeMoss Foundation, 1986) p. 31.

6. Declaration of Independence, 1776.

7. Henry Halley, *Bible Handbook* (Chicago, IL: 1959) p. 22.

8. Ibid.

9. Colossians 1:16 - "For by him all things were created: things in heaven and on earth, visible and invisible, whether thrones or powers or rulers or authorities; all things were created by and for him." In fact, to be specific, this passage says that Christ, the Son of God, did the creating (see also John 1:13; Hebrews 1:2) and holds everything together by the power of His word.

3

He has a vested interest in everything He created including civil government and politics. It would be against His Divine nature to be irresponsibily neglectful of any area of His creation, especially such a critical area as politics. Why? Because the major enslaving force in the history of mankind has been civil governments. Even when people who have been enslaved were not made slaves directly by their government, their slavemasters depended upon the consent of government or at least a looking-the-other-way attitude from the governing authorities.

Since God commands His children not to become the slaves of men,[10] God takes an interest in what goes on in the political arena and expects His children to do the same. Besides, almost one thousand Christians die every day for this faith somewhere in the world.[11] Most of these deaths occur because of governing authorities. To a Christian, it shouldn't matter how far away those people are or the color of their skin. What matters is that another part of the body of Christ (His church) is hurting. And when one part hurts, all parts hurt.[12] And what hurts American Christians most is that their own government is being used to become the major persecuting force against God's people and God's principles at home and abroad (see later chapters).

The Bible vividly illustrates that only a society which secures God's blessing will see its old people at ease and children playing in the streets.[13] Being faithful to God and His ways brings fruitful farms, plenteous harvests, peace in the land, and victory over our enemies.[14] Being unfaithful brings famine, sickness, anxiety, loss of children, attack from foreign armies, scarcity, rationing, and God's hostility.[15]

10. 1 Corinthians 7:23 - "You were bought at a price; do not become slaves of men."

11. "Pioneer," Good News Publishers, Sept.-Oct. 1987, Number 151, quoting missions expert David Barrett, editor of the World Christian Encyclopedia.

12. 1 Corinthians 12:25,26 - "so that there should be no division in the body, but that its parts should have equal concern for each other. If one part suffers, every part suffers with it; if one part is honored, every part rejoices with it."

13. Zechariah 8:1-5.

14. Leviticus 26:3-6.

15. Leviticus 26:41-43.

4

God has these and many more reasons for keeping governments in their proper role. And what might that role be? To protect! To provide justice! In both the Old and New Testaments of the Bible, God says that His purpose for government was a protective, negative role instead of a providing, positive role. The purpose for not giving government the responsibility to provide womb-to-tomb benefits is obvious. Before a government can give something to one citizen, it has to take it from another. Of course, when men use government to take, it is not called "stealing," it is called "socialism," "excessive taxation," deficit spending" or "inflation."

Through the prophet Jeremiah, God told the government of Judah to:

> Do what is just and right. Rescue from the hand of his oppressor the one who has been robbed. Do no wrong or violence to the alien, the fatherless or the widow, and do not shed innocent blood in this place.[16]

Through Paul, God told the Christians in the First Century's world capital of Rome:

> For rulers hold no terror for those who do right, but for those who do wrong. Do you want to be free from fear of the one in authority? Then do what is right and he will commend you. For he is God's servant to do you good. But if you do wrong, be afraid, for he does not bear the sword for nothing. He is God's servant, an agent of wrath to bring punishment on the wrongdoer.[17]

What do we want from government? We want just enough federal government to protect us from international thugs, and to carry out the few responsibilities authorized by the Constitution. All other legitimate functions of government ought to be carried out on the lowest level possible (i.e., state, county, community). But most of all, we want government to administer God's vengeance on anyone who wrongs another. If government does not live up to this vital God-given responsibility, then people begin to take the law into their own hands. When that happens, most nations justify greater government control over everyone's lives and the result is the loss of

16. Jeremiah 22:3.   17. Romans 13:3,4

5

freedom (more on this in a later chapter).

The bottom line here seems to be that a free people need the least amount of government necessary to fulfill its God-given tasks — and no more. After all, rights don't come from government. They come from God. "...all men are...endowed by their Creator with certain unalienable rights..."[18]

God does not divorce politics and religion and He does not want His children to do so. After all, who has the greater responsibility to carry His principles into the political arena? Those who believe in Him or those who do not? The Earth we inhabit is the chessboard for the greatest spiritual warfare of the ages. God broke mankind up into nations that they might seek Him, and Satan keeps drawing men toward a new world order with a world government that man might rebel against God and make a name for himself.

The Bible-believing Christian is called to do battle against spiritual wickedness in high places.[19] And, the Bible-believing Christian is best equipped to do battle against spiritual wickedness in high places.[20] He understands that he is charged with the difficult task of fighting a spiritual war in the physical world.

Every law establishes and legislates morality. What today's critics are saying is, "We don't want God to have anything to do with today's morality. We want to determine what is right and wrong without God. You are welcome to debate right and wrong until you cite a Higher Authority, and then you are automatically disqualified from the debate.

It is no accident that America has moved from George Washington's "It is impossible to rightly govern the world without God and the Bible," to today's humanistic view that insists "you can't legislate morality." Not at all. What is happening is that America has become the battleground between the world's two oldest religions. The first religion to appear in the history of mankind worships God. The second worships man. In America, the first is expressed primarily by Christianity. The second by humanism.

Every book written, every movie produced, every song sung, and every law passed upholds and promotes either one religion

18. Declaration of Independence.   20. Ephesians 6:13-18.
19. Ephesians 6:12.

6

or the other. Think about the last television show you watched or the last song you heard. Look at today's newspaper or your child's school book. Check out the latest law enacted or the most recent Supreme Court decision. God was either recognized as the Creator or ignored; man was either recognized as the created or deified.

It is not a question of whether politics and religion will be mixed. It's a question of which religion will be mixed with American politics. Will it be a religion that worships God, or a religion that worships man? And it is not a question of whether morality can or should be legislated. It is a question of which religious guidelines will undergird the legislation: religious guidelines that deify God, or religious guidelines that deify man?

King David had two hundred advisors who were helpful to him for two primary reasons: 1) They understood God's standards; 2) they understood the times in which they lived.[21] Similarly, God's people today are preparing themselves to be useful to their God and to their government. We have not received a spirit of timidity from God, but a spirit of power and love and self-discipline.[22] We have clothed ourselves in love, which is the perfect bond of unity.[23] We know how to hate the ruler of the darkness of this world and his deceitful schemes without hating the flesh and blood human agents who have been taken captive through false philosophy and deception.[24] Besides, true patriotism doesn't require one to curse his persecutors, but to bless them[25] — whether the blessings are well-received or not.

This would be a good place to discuss another myth that has been as neutralizing to the Christian community as "politics and religion don't mix." Simply stated, it holds that "you can't legislate morality." "Morality" is defined as the condition of conforming with right principles. It pits right against wrong. To "legislate" means to make a law. Law imposes rules of conduct and enforces them with authority. What law has

21. I Chronicles 12:32.
22. 2 Timothy 1:7.
23. Colossians 3:14.
24. Colossians 2:8.
25. Romans 12:14 - "Bless those who persecute you; bless and do not curse."

7

ever been enacted by any government in the history of mankind that has not named something wrong and its opposite right?

How strange that America's "valley of decision" brings her all the way back to Satan's original temptation to deny God and deify mankind. Once again, man is being persuaded to dump God's principles and build his house on a different foundation. America's humanists deny that Satan exists. Sadly, they are proving to be the best disciples he has ever had in the history of mankind.

It is not surprising that Satan would be interested in such a prize plum as the United States of America. For over two hundred years most of America's political leaders have honored God. Look at what our leaders of the past have said about America's tradition of worshiping God and following the Bible:

George Washington: "Whereas it is the duty of all nations to acknowledge the providence of Almighty God, to obey His will, to be grateful for His benefits, and humbly implore His protection and favor...."[26]

Benjamin Franklin: "God governs in the affairs of men."[27]

Andrew Jackson: "That book, sir, is the rock on which our republic rests."[28]

Noah Webster: "The moral principles and precepts contained in the Scriptures ought to form the basis of all our civil constitutions and laws. All the miseries and evils which men suffer from vice, crime, ambition, injustice, oppression, slavery and war, proceed from their despising or neglecting the precepts contained in the Bible."[29]

Horace Greeley: "It is impossible to enslave mentally or socially a Bible-reading people. The principles of the Bible are the groundwork of human freedom."[30]

Emma Willard (1843): "The government of the United States is acknowledged by the wise and good of other nations, to be the most free, impartial, and righteous govern-

26. George Washington's first "Thanksgiving Proclamation," as quoted by Rus Walton, op. cit., p. 32.

27. Benjamin Franklin, as quoted by Rus Walton, op. cit., p. 31.

28. Henry Halley, op. cit., p. 23.

29. Rus Walton, op. cit., p. 33.

30. Henry Halley, op. cit., p. 22.

ment of the world; but all agree, that for such a government to be sustained many years, the principles of truth and righteousness, taught in the Holy Scriptures, must be practiced."[31]

Abraham Lincoln: "It is the duty of nations, as well as of men, to own their dependence upon the overruling power of God and to recognize the sublime truth announced in the Holy Scriptures and proven by all history, that those nations only are blessed whose God is the Lord."[32]

The United States Senate (1863): "Whereas, the Senate of the United States, devoutly recognizing the Supreme Authority and just Government of Almighty God, in all the affairs of men and of nations, has, by a resolution, requested the President to designate and set apart a day for National prayer and humiliation...."[33]

U.S. Grant: "The Bible is the sheet-anchor of our liberties."[34]

Supreme Court decision (1892): "Our laws and our institutions must necessarily be based upon and embody the teachings of the Redeemer of mankind. It is impossible that it should be otherwise; and in this sense and to this extent our civilization and our institutions are emphatically Christian...."[35]

Even foreigners have recognized which choice of religions America made:

Alexis De Tocqueville (1840): "I sought for the key to the greatness and genius of America in her harbors....; in her fertile fields and boundless forests; in her rich mines and vast world commerce; in her public school system and institutions of learning. I sought for it in her democratic Congress and in her matchless Constitution.

31. Emma Willard, 1843, *Teaching and Learning America's Christian History* (San Francisco, CA: Foundation for American Christian Education, 1975), compiled by Verna M. Hall, p.xi.

32. Rus Walton, op. cit., p. 32

33. "Proclamation Appointing a National Fast Day," U.S. Senate, March 30, 1863, cited in *A Nation Under God?*, C.E. Galalivan, Ed., (Waco, TX: Word Books, 1976) p. 19.

34. Henry Halley, op. cit., p. 36.

35. Supreme Court decision, 1892, Church of the "Holy Trinity vs. United States," quoted by Rus Walton, op cit., p. 21.

Not until I went into the churches of America and heard her pulpits flame with righteousness did I understand the secret of her genius and power. America is great because America is good, and if America ever ceases to be good, America will cease to be great."[36]

Charles Malik, former Lebanese Ambassador to the United Nations (1950s): "The good (in the United States) would never have come into being without the blessing and the power of Jesus Christ....I know how embarrassing this matter is to politicians, bureaucrats, businessmen and cynics; but, whatever these honored men think, the irrefutable truth is that the soul of America is at its best and highest, Christian."[37]

So, what went wrong? How did America get from there to here? From a Christian nation to a humanist nation? From worshiping God to worshiping man? From the Supreme Court decision of 1892 (see above) to the Supreme Court decision of 1963 (banning prayer and Bible reading in schools)? From individualism to collectivism? From morality to immorality and then amorality?

Was all of this an accident? Did things simply follow a natural course, or did someone make them happen? Was there a plan? What is it? Who would purposely do such a thing? What are their names? Have they formed organizations? Have they published their views? Where can I find them? Why don't our media tell us about this? Are our elected officials in on this? Where can I get their voting record based on these issues? Can anything moral and legal be done to stop this spiritual and political trashing of America? What is it? Who is already doing something about this? What are they doing? What can I do? Is it too late?

These and other questions are the basis for the rest of this book.

36. Alexis De Tocqueville, as quoted in *The New American,* December 12, 1986, p. 10.

37. Charles Malik, as quoted by Rus Walton, op. cit., p. 21.

"With cunning they conspire against your [God's] people; they plot against those you cherish. 'Come,' they say, 'let us destroy them as a nation...'" Psalm 83:3-4a

— 2 —
NONE DARE CALL IT CONSPIRACY

I do. And so did the late Gary Allen in a book by that title which sold millions of copies during the presidential election year of 1972.[1] Why is it so hard for people to see conspiracy behind the radical changes in America? What does the word "conspiracy" mean, anyway?

"Conspiracy" is a deliberate plot to do evil; an agreement among several persons to do something evil; two or more persons acting in harmony to accomplish an evil purpose.

Is it evil to maneuver America from deifying God to deifying man? Does it take more than one person? Then there's conspiracy.

Is it evil to socialize America? Does it take more than one person working in harmony to set up this system of legal plunder? Then there's conspiracy.

Is it evil to aid Communism? Does it take more than one person to spend $700 million of taxpayers' money to pay Communist Poland's interest on its national debt? Then there's conspiracy.

Is it evil to fill school children's minds with amoral sex education in our government schools? Does it take more than one person to design the programs, print the textbooks, and force our local teachers to teach our innocent children that homosexuality is simply an alternate lifestyle and that sex before marriage is their own business as long as it's "safe" (by

1. Gary Allen, *None Dare Call It Conspiracy* (Seal Beach, CA: Concord Press, 1971). Still available; purchase by sending $3.00 to General Birch Services, 395 Concord Ave., Belmont, MA 02178.

"safe" they mean you don't get a disease or get pregnant)? Then there's conspiracy.

The Bible-believing Christian, especially, does not have a problem believing that conspiracies exist. The Bible warns about the schemes of the Devil,[2] tells us that he is the father of lies,[3] and that he masquerades himself as an angel of light.[4]

We know that there was a conspiracy to crucify Christ.[5] The Old Testament says that Absalom's conspiracy was strong to overthrow his father's throne,[6] that the king of Assyria found conspiracy in Hoshea,[7] and that certain government officials in Babylon conspired against Daniel to discredit him before the king.[8]

Absalom cloaked his conspiracy to overthrow his father's throne with promises of better justice to everyone who had received an unfavorable decision in King David's court. He told them that if he had been their judge, he would have decided in their favor. Also, when they bowed down to Absalom, he would quickly lift them up and treat them as an equal. Of course, he was only cloaking his goal of accumulating power for evil purposes with a claim that the people would benefit. All conspirators have to do this in order to get non-conspiratorial hands to help them accomplish their evil goals. The Bible says that he stole away the hearts of God's people and they helped him overthrow King David. Once in power, Absalom dropped the cloak and began a reign of terror.

When two or more people get together and plot evil, there is conspiracy. And the first rule for all conspiracies, great or small, is to keep their plot hidden as long as possible. Obviously you can't have a conspiracy if everybody knows about it.

Besides, if conspirators keep their evil motives hidden then it

2. Ephesians 6:11.

3. John 8:44 - "You belong to your father, the devil, and you want to carry out your father's desire. He was a murderer from the beginning, not holding to the truth, for there is no truth in him. When he lies, he speaks his native language, for he is a liar and the father of lies."

4. 2 Corinthians 11:14,15 - "And no wonder, for Satan himself masquerades as an angel of light."

5. Mark 14:1.

6. 2 Samuel 15:12.

7. 2 Kings 17:4.

8. Daniel 6:1-28.

appears to the general populace that nothing more is involved than a debating match between two opinions. When the proponents of one side aren't playing by the rules but make it appear that they are, they obviously have a great advantage. A preacher friend of mine, Riley Donica, tells about an experience he had in high school that illustrates this very well. It seems that the boys at his high school would put on boxing gloves and fill their lunch hour with boxing matches. On one occasion, an older boy challenged Riley to put on the gloves, but suggested that they only spar instead of actually fighting. Riley says, "I sparred, but he fought. I was pulling my punches and he was hitting me with everything he had. I looked pretty bad and took a beating that day."[9]

That's what has been happening for a hundred years in American politics. God's people have been pulling their punches while the other side has been flailing away. Most American Christians have had a hard time believing that other Americans could be so evil as to purposely cause wars, wage wars for political purposes, lose wars purposely, aid the other side while our fighting men are dying on the battlefield daily, sink their own national sovereignty to prepare America to be just another province in a world government, promote collectivism and amorality in order to prepare America for a new world order, destroy the family and true religion in order to break down the final barriers of opposition, and purposely undermine the most rewarding economic system that working people and the poor have experienced in the history of mankind all just to create the chaos needed to stampede an entire nation into demanding its own slavery.

Bible-reading Christians, of all people, aren't surprised that men can be so evil. Even if Hollywood excuses the cruel crucifixion of Jesus as simply the reaction of politically-minded men who felt their power over the people threatened, how do you explain the slaughter of those innocent babies in Bethlehem unless you acknowledge that men can be so evil?[10] What had those babies or their parents done to deserve that? Are we to blame God? No! An evil government official con-

9. Riley says the next time the older boy challenged him to a "sparring" match, he accepted...and whipped the tar out of him.

10. Matthew 2:1-18.

spired to do this. Conspired? Yes, conspired! Remember, conspirators hide their real purposes. Herod told the wise men who were seeking the Christ-Child, "When you have found Him, report to me, that I too may come and worship Him." Horse feathers! He didn't want to worship the Christ-Child. He wanted to kill Him. But the wise men believed Herod. After all, he sounded so sincere and he was a king. Besides, nobody could be that evil. It took a special warning from God to keep them from going back to Herod and, in their political innocence, telling him exactly where to find Jesus.

There's no room here for the accidental view of history. Those babies did not die by accident. Those soldiers didn't accidentally kill those babies. And it's no accident that America has arrived at the point of slaughtering as many innocent babies every hour of every day for the past fifteen years as were slaughtered in Bethlehem on that one occasion.

The Bible says there are people who delight in doing evil,[11] who cannot sleep unless they do evil,[12] who excel in deeds of wickedness,[13] who devise evil continually,[14] and who "love evil rather than good, falsehood rather than speaking the truth."[15] Why did we think that America would escape from ever having such evil men? And did we think that all evil men would live on the wrong side of the tracks and look like hoodlums or come from another country? What is wrong with Americans that we can't imagine that someone with higher education, wearing a three-piece suit, and making sizable contributions to charities could not also be plotting to work some horrible evil upon his fellow-countrymen and all mankind?

After a hundred years of the virtual absence of born-again Christians from the American political arena, what can we expect to have happened? Who did we expect would be minding the store? Who did we expect would maintain God's principles in the political arena, God's enemies? Did we think Satan's crowd would be asleep at the switch and pass up an opportunity to lead America down a path toward slavery? And then,

11. Proverbs 2:14,15.
12. Proverbs 4:16, 17.
13. Jeremiah 5:25-29.
14. Proverbs 6:14.
15. Psalm 52:3.

14

while America was still enjoying the reputation of a God-fearing, freedom-loving land, turning her into the world's primary exporter of collectivism and amorality? And did we think that the conspirators would welcome our return to what had become their domain? Did we expect them to rejoice that we decided once again to wrestle against spiritual wickedness in high places, against the rulers of the darkness of this world?[16]

The old techniques that had worked to make a century of Christians so heavenly minded that they were no earthly good simply stopped working. A revival had begun to sweep the nation that not only touched the spirit of man, but also affected his entire life. Suddenly, it wasn't enough to be a Christian only within the four walls of a church building.

Believers were discovering in their Bibles a God who was concerned with every area of His creation and demanded of His children that they be concerned too.

And what had prepared the hearts of men for this revival? Probably the severity of the problems we faced. The war on the family by our own government, the loss of local control over the education of our children, a couple of no-win wars and the ensuing loss of confidence that everything was going okay in Washington, the legalization and then the actual promotion of abortion and homosexuality, the unbelievable extent of our aid and trade with a Communist empire that was shrinking the free world daily, the obviously manipulated economic upheavals that were taking the control of the wealth of the nation out of the hands of the people, and the near destruction of a generation of American youth by removal of morality from their education and entertainment, replacing it with the destructive philosophies of amorality and immorality.

The late FBI director, J. Edgar Hoover, said, "...the individual is handicapped by coming face to face with a conspiracy so monstrous (that) he cannot believe it exists." But as Bible-believing Christians studied their Bibles, their eyes were beginning to open not just to the evil that men do but also to the secret schemes that evil men use (especially in government).

The prophet Micah wrote:

> Woe to those who plan iniquity, to those who

---

16. Ephesians 6:12.

plot evil on their beds! At morning's light they carry it out because it is in their power to do it. They covet fields and seize them, and houses, and take them. They defraud a man of his home, a fellowman of his inheritance.[17]

David's prayer about those who conspired against his nation makes a perfect prayer for today's Christian in America:

Hide me from the conspiracy of the wicked, from the noisy crowd of evildoers, who sharpen their tongues like swords and aim their words like deadly arrows. They shoot from ambush at the innocent man: they shoot at him suddenly, without fear. They encourage each other in evil plans, they talk about hiding their snares; they say, "Who will see them?" They plot injustice and say, "We have devised a perfect plan!" Surely the mind and heart of man are cunning.[18]

Of course, as before, God's people are tempted to retreat from concern about the political arena with neutralizing arguments such as: "Your citizenship is in heaven," "Don't get entangled in the affairs of everyday life," and "You shouldn't even speak the things done in darkness." But today's believer is sharper and more discerning. He looks up phrases like these in the Bible and checks to see if they have been used out of context. He finds that the first quote[19] was written by the apostle Paul (by inspiration of the Holy Spirit). Paul didn't hesitate to use his earthly (Roman) citizenship to get out of unfair scrapes with the law.[20] He had no problem integrating his heavenly and earthly citizenships. The second phrase[21] was written by that same apostle. He didn't hesitate to "entangle" himself in such affairs of everyday life as working to support himself when necessary[22] and teaching about the proper role of government.[23] His warning was directed at those who would

17. Micah 2:1-2.
18. Psalm 64:2-6.
19. Philippians 3:20.
20. Acts 16:37-38; 22:25-29; 25:10-12.
21. 2 Timothy 2:4.
22. Acts 20:34,35.
23. Romans 13:1-7.

run from the spiritual war that surrounds us all. The third neutralizing phrase[24] is drawn from the passage which, in context, teaches Christians not to participate in deeds of darkness and then actually commands them to expose deeds of darkness with the light of Christ.

Today's Christians are more aware of their total life's responsibility to serve God. They are more willing to be the light of the world[25] and the salt of the earth.[26] Today's Christian sees himself as a holy and royal priest[27] with one foot in the spiritual realm and the other still in the physical realm serving as God's bridge to mankind and mankind's bridge to God. Today's Christian realizes that God has principles for the political arena and if he doesn't carry them into that arena, nobody will.

God isn't so weak that He can't stamp out evil whenever he chooses. But have you noticed that God usually chooses to move ahead only when He has a human agent through whom he can work? Through the prophet Ezekiel, God said He was looking for at least one person to stand in the gap for the land.[28] Isaiah said God was astonished that He couldn't find a single person among His people to intercede for them.[29] God told the Israelites entering the promised land that He had given them the battle but it remained for them to wage it.[30] God drove out His enemies only as His people were willing to move forward and occupy. God needs more believers who are willing to stand in the gap for their families, their communities, and their country. Today's astute Christian has no mistaken vision of conquering government to force everyone to be religious. He seeks only to see that government provides its proper function: to protect life and property and administer justice.

God is in no way defeated because someone appears to have successfully schemed against Him and His principles. He told

24. Ephesians 5:12.

25. Matthew 5:14.

26. Matthew 5:13.

27. 1 Peter 2:5,9.

28. Ezekiel 22:30 - "I looked for a man among them who would build up the wall and stand before me in the gap on behalf of the land so I would not have to destroy it, but I found none."

29. Isaiah 59:16.

30. Deuteronomy 9:23.

17

one king who schemed against Him, "...I know where you stay and when you come and go and how you rage against Me."[31] Equally, God's people are not surprised and do not feel defeated that God's enemies would oppose them. Jesus warned that His followers would be hated just as He had been.[32]

So, today's Bible-believing Christian is aware that evil men organize and conspire against God's ways. He knows that they can best be identified by taking note of who opposes God's principles; that they are not guided by any sense of nobility and will use any ruthless means to oppose God's guidelines; that they must keep their evil plot hidden to suceed and can be effectively fought only through exposure; that they often cloak their accumulation of power for evil purposes with claims that mankind will benefit from their schemes; that they try to neutralize their potential Christian opposition, even twisting scripture for this purpose; that they depend upon non-conspiratorial hands to help them accomplish their evil purposes; and that while God's power can stop them and restore freedom, He will use it only when and where He can find men willing to stand in the gap with His principles.

Now let us look at Satan's conspiracy against God's principles in America.

31. 2 Kings 19:27.
32. John 15:18-20.

"As one seeks to honor one's family he will seek to protect it, affirm it, preserve it....He will criticize and fight the politicians who, in their own greed and for their own power, seek to destroy the family."

— *E. Merrill Root*[1]

— 3 —

THE CONSPIRACY AGAINST THE AMERICAN FAMILY

As a professional marriage and family counselor, I became excited at the opportunity to attend a "Conference on the Family" sponsored by one of my professional associations. Once there, however, I sat in shocked disbelief as the opening speaker applauded the death of the traditional American family. What followed the next three days was even more alarming. Traditional faith was viewed as harmful. Abortion was promoted and categorized merely as a means of birth control. Homosexuality was defended as an alternative lifestyle. Parental authority was undermined. Moral values were held to be autonomous (do your own thing) and situational (right and wrong are never absolutes; situations determine rightness and wrongness). Public education exists to channel a generation of youth into "more enlightened" living. And expansion of the size, scope and power of the federal government would solve every problem of mankind without creating any new ones.

Throughout history, evil men have conspired to enslave free people. Their plans have always had a common goal: destroy the family. Until the family government is undermined, the right climate to overthrow a freedom-based civil government is impossible.

Family is where life makes up its mind. Unless the family is weakened, morals stay strong. Strong families tend to teach

1. E. Merrill Root, *America's Steadfast Dream* (Boston, MA: Western Islands, 1977), p. 270.

and perpetuate a strong religious faith. Good families, strong morality, and faith in God have always been the absolute enemies of tyranny. So, it is not surprising where the battle-lines between freedom and slavery are drawn. Here are some historical examples outlining plans for overthrowing a free people.

Cleon Skousen tells us that in *The Republic* (circa Fourth Century B.C.),

> Plato's "ideal" society included the elimination of marriage and the family so that all the women would belong to all the men and all the men would belong to all the women. Children resulting from these pro-miscuous unions would be taken over by the govern-ment as soon as they were weaned and raised anonymously by the state. Plato wanted women to be required to be equal with men — to fight wars with the men and perform labor like men. There was to be selective breeding of men and women under control of the government and children considered inferior or crippled were to be destroyed.[2]

On May 1, 1776, Adam Weishaupt established an ambitious conspiratorial plan to rule the world. Quickly penetrating the academic communities at the universities in Germany, and rapidly spreading into France, his Illuminati was largely responsible for the French Revolution and the terror from which France has never really recovered. The goals of the Il-luminati included: The obliteration of Christianity and the renunciation of all religion; the deification of sensuality; the repudiation of marriage; and the state adoption of children.[3]

Another of the major writings in history detailing plans to enslave a free people is the *Communist Manifesto*. In it, Karl Marx openly called for the abolition of the family! He claimed to want to stop the exploitation of children by their parents. He called for an openly legalized community of women for all men. And, not surprisingly, Marx also called for the abolition

2. Cleon Skousen, *The Naked Capitalist* (Salt Lake City, UT: W. Cleon Skousen, 1970), p. 27.

3. John F. McManus, *"An Overview of Our World,"* The text of a filmstrip produced by The John Birch Society, Belmont, MA, 1971, pp. 50-51.

20

of private property. He recognized how difficult, if not impossible it is to maintain a strong family structure if the right to own private property is eliminated. We shall return to this important subject later in this chapter.

By the time *Humanist Manifesto I* (1933) and *Humanist Manifesto II* (1973) were written, direct calls for the destruction of the family were eliminated, but attitudes which undermine it were presented as inherent rights: the right to suicide, the right to "die with dignity" — euthanasia; and the right to abortion and divorce. The humanists also called for the undermining of parental authority and the replacing of it with governmental authority; open sex (homosexuality, etc.); and the elimination of private property.[4]

The speakers at the conference I attended had one thing in common; they all worshiped at the altar of America's new official religion — humanism. The beliefs of a humanist are interesting to study. It is as if they sat down with the Christian Bible, wrote out every principle, determined the exact opposite of each, and adopted these as their basic doctrine.

Regarding homosexuality, God says it is an abomination,[5] a degrading passion, indecent,[6] and will not be allowed in heaven.[7] Humanism says, "The many varieties of sexual exploration should not in themselves be considered 'evil'."[8]

God says we should be concerned about our relationship with Him as more important than life itself.[9] Humanism says, "Promises of immortal salvation or fear of eternal damnation are both illusory and harmful."[10]

God says He has a divine purpose for each human life; that He is responsible for creating us in His image and will save those who come to Him through His son, Jesus.[11] Humanism says, "We can discover no divine purpose or providence for the human species. While there is much we do not know,

4. *Humanist Manifesto I & II,* Paul Kurtz, Ed. (Buffalo, NY: Prometheus Books, 1973), pp. 9-20.

5. Leviticus 18:22.

6. Romans 1:26, 27.

7. 1 Corinthians 6:9-11

8. *Humanist Manifesto I & II,* p. 18.

9. Matthew 4:4.

10. *Humanist Manifesto I & II,* p.16

11. Psalm 139:16; Genesis 1:26; John 1:12.

humans are responsible for what we are or will become. No diety will save us; we must save ourselves."[12]

Let me assure you that I am not making this up. A prominent group of humanists in 1933, and another even larger group in 1973 published their beliefs in the aforementioned *Humanist Manifesto I* and *Humanist Manifesto II*. Dozens of educators, publishers, writers, political activists, ministers, scientists, and industrial leaders endorsed these documents. Millions more follow them. In fact, humanism has become the exclusive religious influence in government, education, entertainment, media, and politics. Promoting humanism is the major way to advance in public education, to make it big in entertainment, to get recognition in media, or to survive in the political arena.

Of course, today's humanism in America is European Marxism warmed over and given a less controversial name. Marxism called for the destruction of not only the family, but also of God-centered religion, morality, private property, and all independent governments in order to establish a new world order under a world government.

In America, whenever the public began to become aware of the nature of Marxism, socialism and communism, the conspirators disguised their plans by calling instead for the New Deal, progressive education, Keynesian economics, the New Morality, the Great Society, and humanism.

Let us now document the philosophical attack by humanism on the American family and expose the special interest organizations that are directly doing the attacking. Their weapons are homosexuality, abortion, government education, humanistic religion, and socialism.

HOMOSEXUALITY

Those who conspire against a free people have no better weapon for destroying the traditional family than the promotion of homosexuality. Homosexuality is such an offense to God that the Law of Moses given to the Israelite nation called for the death penalty for those who were homosexuals.[13] Some

---

12. *Humanist Manifesto I & II*, p.16.

13. Leviticus 20:13 - "If a man lies with a man as one lies with a woman, both of them have done what is detestable. They must be put to death; their blood will be in their own heads."

argue that since that command is in the Old Testament, homosexuality is acceptable in the New Testament. Nothing could be further from the truth. The New Testament leaves no doubt about how God continues to feel about homosexuality.

> Because of this, God gave them over to shameful lusts. Even their women exchanged natural relations for unnatural ones. In the same way the men also abandoned natural relations with women and were inflamed with lust for one another. Men committed indecent acts with other men, and received in themselves the due penalty for their perversion.
>
> Romans 1:26, 27

God says, "All other sins a man commits are outside his body, but he who sins sexually sins against his own body."[14] Sexual diseases have ravaged man for as long as there has been sexual immorality. The Bible-believing Christian is not surprised that as soon as man thinks he has outsmarted God by finding a treatment for all known sexual diseases, along comes a new disease even harder to treat than the last one. While no Bible-believing Christian is opposed to medical science trying to discover another secret of healing from God's creation (after all, innocent people are always hurt by the outrages of others), he is not surprised that science is unable to find a permanent way to bypass God's eternal truths of right and wrong. Just as it was true that "All the king's horses and all the king's men couldn't put Humpty Dumpty together again," all the scientists and governments who rail against God and His absolutes can't make sexual perversion acceptable. But then, that's not the humanists' real purpose. Their real goal is to destroy morality and the family, and then build a new world order on the ashes of their destruction.

Bible-believing Christians are not amazed at the incredible promiscuity of today's homosexual because the first book of the Bible tells how unbelievably promiscuous homosexuals were thousands of years ago. When the two angels disguised as men visited righteous Lot in the wicked city of Sodom (from which our language derives the legal term "sodomy" — when was the the last time you heard anyone in the media call

14. 1 Corinthians 6:18b.

homosexuality by its legal name?), the men of Sodom said to Lot, "Where are the men who came to you tonight? Bring them out to us so that we can have sex with them."[15] Studies on today's homosexuals have found that those who contract the dread disease called AIDS average 1,100 sexual partners over their lifetimes. Being "gay", as opposed to simply being homosexual (according to the "gay" community), is a matter of having a large number of sexual contacts.[16]

The Bible tells us that "all the men from every part of the city of Sodom — both young and old — surrounded the house."[17] Now we know "the rest of the story:" the men of Sodom were not just homosexual, they were "gay." They had engaged in perverted sexual practices with each other so often that when a new man came to town, they all lined up demanding to have sex with him. If you really want to know what God thinks of homosexuality, look at Sodom's penalty: "Then the Lord rained down burning sulfur on Sodom and Gomorrah — from the Lord out of the heavens. Thus he overthrew those cities and the entire plain, including all those living in the cities — and also the vegetation in the land."[18] The New Testament says, "Sodom and Gomorrah and the surrounding towns gave themselves up to sexual immorality and perversion. They serve as an example of those who suffer the punishment of eternal fire."[19]

What happened to Sodom was God's proof that there is an eternal punishment. Bible-believing Christians suspect that what is happening to today's sodomites as a result of AIDS is a modern-day example that God still has an eternal judgment. We rejoice at the number of homosexuals who are repenting of their sins and are turning to Christ before they die of AIDS. We applaud those churches and groups who are counseling and reforming homosexuals, especially those with AIDS.

Homosexuals are not to be hated even though they have brought this disease to non-homosexuals. Homosexuals are often portrayed as AIDS "victims." They are not victims, they

15. Genesis 19:5.
16. *The New American,* August 31, 1987, pp. 31-32.
17. Genesis 19:4.
18. Genesis 29:24, 25.
19. Jude 7.

are perpetrators. Blood transfusion recipients and newborn babies infected with AIDS are the victims!

Our nation's government and the media are working overtime to keep the public from blaming homosexuals for AIDS. A recent newsletter from a congressman entitled *"AIDS: Some Questions and Answers"* failed to mention homosexuality one single time in the text of the entire newsletter.[20] This is exactly the approach homosexual groups have taken for years, steadfastly refusing to accept the linkage between their perverted lifestyle and AIDS. In the newsletter, a pie-shaped graph which illustrates adult patient groups with AIDS finally mentions the word homosexual. At that point we learn that 74 percent of all reported adult cases of AIDS from 1981 until February, 1987 were homosexual/bisexual men and 17 percent were I.V. drug users who were not homosexual. Unless my old math fails me, that's a whopping 91 percent of the total cases reported. Transfusion recipients make up 2 percent, heterosexuals 4 percent, hemophiliacs 1 percent, and undetermined causes were 3 percent. And remember, in most cases, a health official was not involved at the time this information was gathered. It's likely that some of the heterosexual AIDS cases were homosexuals who refused to admit they were.

Most homosexual (sodomy) laws have not been enforced for years, and some have been quietly taken off the statute books. Meanwhile, pro-homosexual (gay rights) groups have gained such political clout that the National March on Washington for Lesbian and Gay Rights in October, 1987 was endorsed by two U.S. Senators, 29 U.S. Representatives, 9 mayors, 7 cities, and 21 organizations other than homosexual and AIDS organizations.[21] *The New American* magazine noted that the march ended with a rally at the Capitol, featuring a keynote speech by Jesse Jackson.[22]

This is our "valley of decision," America. If we do absolutely nothing, we stand to lose our families and our freedom to these militant homosexuals. We must do something to stop

20. *"A Special Anthony Health Report,"* Beryl Anthony, 4th District, Ark., October, 1987.

21. Kirk Kidwell, "Front Page — The Politics of Perversion," *The New American,* November 9, 1987, p. 9.

22. Kidwell, op. cit., p. 9.

them. Politicians who refuse to oppose homosexuality either have sold out to humanism or they have both eyes on the next election and fear the combined political wrath of homosexuals, other humanists and a liberal media gone mad.

The liberal media is not the only place where madness reigns. Our federal government gave $674,679 it had taken from us in taxes to the Gay Men's Health Crisis in New York City. The Gay Men's Health Crisis then published a "safe-sex" comic book which, in the condemning words of Senator Jesse Helms, "...promotes sodomy and the homosexual lifestyle as an acceptable alternative in American society."[23] Homosexuality will continue to engulf America as a result of these kinds of humanistic, tax-supported educational programs.

Don't forget, the purpose of Satan's crowd is not to stop the spread of the deadly disease called AIDS, but to use it to stampede an otherwise reasonable people into countenancing the growth and outreach of government until there exists total government control over everything. Humanists will clamor for national health care insurance and then the nationalization (total government control) of the entire health care industry itself. And they will get their way unless enough people wake up soon. The threat of AIDS could be minimized if our nation would oppose homosexuality and its vile practices. Instead, however, the AIDS plague is being used to socialize America. AIDS is the first politically protected plague in the history of mankind.

God-fearing and Bible-believing Americans should oppose all educational activities that fail to link homosexuality with AIDS. We should reject all materials teaching that there is any "safe sex" other than abstinence from sexual activity outside a sexually monogamous and heterosexual marriage. And we must also oppose all programs that teach anything less than total abstinence from the use of illegal drugs. Opposing only illegal intravenous drugs ignores the fact that most individuals who use intravenous drugs started with non-intravenous drugs.

Legally called upon to act on behalf of homosexuals is the American Civil Liberties Union (ACLU) which endorses child custody rights for gays. Founded in 1920 by a group that in-

23. Kirk Kidwell, "Nation/Capitol Update — Legislative Aids," *The New American,* November 23, 1987, p. 11.

26

cluded well-known Communists William Z. Foster, Elizabeth Gurley Flynn and Harry Ward, the Civil Liberties Union has always worked to tear away the very foundation of liberty: God-centered morality and religion. When the ACLU defends a supposed right, some more bulwarks of our civilization are threatened, and the vast majority of Americans find themselves less free.

Over the years, the ACLU has waged war against internal security laws, school prayer, restrictions against abortion, community nativity scenes, and capital punishment for heinous crimes. When challenged to assist millions of Americans who want relief from being forced to finance morally and educationally deficient government schools, the ACLU was not interested.

Instead, the organization has spent considerable effort defending the interests of pornographers, drug pushers and other elements of the counter-culture in our nation.

For more than 50 years until his death in 1981, the ACLU's top official was Roger Baldwin. He spelled out his own goals in 1935 as follows:

> I am for socialism, disarmament and ultimately for abolishing the State itself as an instrument of violence and compulsion. I seek the social ownership of property, the abolition of the propertied class, and the sole control of those who produce wealth. Communism is the goal.

Far from defending true liberty, the ACLU has always functioned as an extension of the Baldwin aims.

In addition to using homosexuality, those who conspire against the family promote abortion.

ABORTION

I have never been involved in a military war but I believe General William T. Sherman was correct in 1880 when he said, "War is hell." The wars of this century have cost our nation alone 426,817 soldiers killed in action. If you add in other deaths related to war (accidents, illness), the total rises to a whopping 632,716 deaths. That includes World War I, World War II, the Korean "Police Action" and the Vietnam "Conflict." If you then add the casualties suffered in all the other wars our nation has fought (War of Independence, War of 1812, Mexican War, Civil War, and the Spanish-American War), you will arrive at a grand total of 957,839 war-related deaths.

Think of all the dads who never got to see their youngsters grow up. Think of all the young men who never got to grow up and have their own families. Think of all those who became physically, emotionally and mentally scarred by all these wars.

Then, answer this question for me: In America right now, is it safer to be a young man of military age or a little baby in a mother's womb? Before answering, consider this: In 1987, America's mothers and their cooperating doctors killed more Americans than have perished in all the wars in the history of our country. In any single day — today for instance — more Americans will be killed in our sparkling clean hospitals and clinics than were killed in action in the War for Independence from 1775 to 1783. In the past fourteen days more Americans were legally killed than died in the entire twelve years of the no-win war in Vietnam.

War is certainly hell. But so is abortion. And saying so will get you into a lot of trouble in today's humanist-dominated media and education circles. But the Bible-believing Christian cares what God thinks about abortion. If God is against it, then he is as well.

Perhaps the clearest Bible reference to the worth of the unborn child is found in Psalm 139:13-16:

> For you created my inmost being, you knit me together in my mother's womb. I praise you because I am fearfully and wonderfully made; your works are wonderful, I know that full well. My frame was not hidden from you when I was made in the secret place. When I was woven together in the depths of the earth, your eyes saw my unformed body. All the days ordained for me were written in your book before one of them came to be.

Can you imagine how God feels about those who deliberately kill the unborn? Abortion makes live babies dead. Abortion is the deliberate taking of a human life. Abortion is the murder of an innocent child. According to noted law professor Dr. Charles E. Rice:

...the unborn child is in fact a human being from the moment of conception. When the child in the womb weighs only 1/30th of an ounce, he has every internal organ he will ever have as an adult. On the 18th day after his conception, his heart starts beating. A 18 weeks, he can suck his thumb, scratch himself and even cry.[24]

God certainly seems to value the life of the unborn child differently than He would a woman's appendix or her tonsils. Yet today's humanists claim that a woman's having her appendix cut out and thrown away is no different from having her baby cut out and thrown away.

To what god are we sacrificing 125,000 American babies monthly? To the god of convenience? Yes, and also to the god of the humanist religion that always makes war on God and His ways.

In the war that rages all about us, there are those who uphold God's ways and there are those who actively oppose them. But there is a larger segment of mankind who sees what is happening and takes no side. "I have not been responsible for killing any unborn children so God can't be unhappy with me," is an oft-repeated claim. But God says if someone closes his or her eyes to the sacrificing of children and does nothing, He will set His face against that person and his or her family and will cut them off from His people.[25]

If there really is a God, if the Bible really is His revelation to man, then there can be no neutral ground on moral issues. As Jesus said, "He who is not with me is against me and he who does gather with Me scatters;"[26] and "Because you are lukewarm — neither hot or cold — I am about to spit you out of my mouth."[27]

The poet Dante was correct when he said, "The hottest places in hell are reserved for those who, in a period of moral crisis, maintain their neutrality."[28] God will not forgive a na-

---

24. Dr. Charles E. Rice, Prof. of Law at Notre Dame University, author of *The Vanishing Right To Live.*

25. Leviticus 20:1-5.

26. Matthew 12:30.

27. Revelation 3:16.

28. Dante Alighieri (1265-1321).

tion for soaking its own soil with innocent blood.[29] A nation cannot survive when it permits horrible sinfulness to go unpunished.

How did America get to the point of being so highly offensive to God? Did this happen by accident? No, how can anyone claim that a nation accidentally swings from individualism and morality to collectivism and moral anarchy? It is no accident when evil men sharpen their skills at undermining the family and enslaving a free people for several generations.

America's morality has not sunk to great depths by accident but by design. Let us look at a small sampling of the influences responsible for America's genocide against the unborn: the U.S. Supreme Court and the Planned Parenthood Federation.

U.S. Supreme Court

On January 22, 1973, the Supreme Court of the United States decided, by a vote of seven to two, that abortion would henceforth be legal throughout the United States. The belief that the Court sanctioned the practice only in the first three months of pregnancy is a myth. As the Senate Judiciary Committee explained nine years later, "no significant legal barriers of any kind whatsoever exist today in the United States for a woman to obtain an abortion for any reason during any stage of pregnancy." Since 1973, additional Supreme Court decisions have struck down virtually all attempts to minimize the slaughter of 1.5 million unborn infants each year.

One of the most revealing aspects of the Supreme Court's action is its reported refusal to address the matter of when life begins. If life begins nine months before birth at conception, then abortion is the taking of an innocent life, or murder. But if life begins at some time after conception, or even at birth itself, then abortion is not murder. The reason why the Court did not address this critical matter is that, if it had, any conclusion other than that life begins at conception would have been medically and scientifically ludicrous. And the Justices knew it. They sanctioned abortion for social and economic reasons in

29. 2 Kings 24:3, 4 - "Surely these things happened to Judah according to the Lord's command, in order to remove them from his presence because of the sins of Manasseh and all he had done, including the shedding of innocent blood. For he had filled Jerusalem with innocent blood, and the Lord was not willing to forgive."

what dissenting Justice Byron R. White called "an exercise of raw judicial power."

The most fundamental purpose for creating a government is to have it protect life. With the abortion decision, the government has instead become a partner in the murder of the most defenseless of human beings, the infant in the womb. If government can sanction the murder of some human beings for social, economic or other reasons, the door is open for sanctioning the murder of others — the aged, the infirm, those with the "wrong" skin color or ethnic background, even those deemed politically or religiously "abrasive."

Planned Parenthood

Founded in 1916 as the Birth Control League of America by Margaret Sanger, the Planned Parenthood Federation of America defines its own role as "making effective means of voluntary fertility control, including contraception, abortion and sterilization fully accessible to all." With national headquarters, regional offices, a network of 188 affiliated offices, *and tens of millions of dollars from federal, state and local governments,* the organization helped as much as any single group to pave the way for the Supreme Court's 1973 abortion-on-demand decision. Since that decision, the organization has performed tens of thousands of abortions each year.

In the spring 1965 issue of *The Humanist,* author Miriam Allen DeFord wrote: "It was the radicals — political, economic, and religious — among whom Margaret Sanger found her first supporters: and she herself was one of them. Her father, Matthew Higgins, was a Socialist and the 'villiage atheist' of Corning, New York."

DeFord explained that the term "humanist" was not being used when Sanger launched her crusade. "But call it Freethought or Rationalism or Secularism, it was and it remained Margaret Sanger's creed. The first paper she founded and edited was called *The Woman Rebel,* and its masthead bore the motto: 'No gods, no masters.'"

Always a fervent advocate of eugenics, the science of controlled breeding, Sanger described a class that included the poor and the religious who wanted large families, and then concluded, "The procreation of this group should be stopped." Continuing this barbarous attitude, Planned Parenthood leader Alan Guttmacker had advocated the use of various compulsory population control measures when needed.

The pro-death mentality let loose by the pro-abortion decision and supported by Planned Parenthood and others must be overturned if we are to expect God's blessings on this nation. And it will be overturned if enough Christians get involved and make their voices heard.

PUBLIC EDUCATION

Nowhere is the battle between Christianity and the godless religion of humanism more evident than in America's public school system. No one doubts the importance of controlling the education of a nation's children. The power to control the content of a nation's textbooks is the power to control the nation's future. C.S. Lewis sent a warning to fellow Christians when he said, "I doubt whether we are sufficiently attentive to the importance of elementary textbooks."[30]

Bible-believing Christians are instructed by God's Holy Word to bring up their children in the discipline and instruction of the Lord.[31] We are told that the fear of the Lord is the beginning of knowledge,[32] and the training of children must include instruction in wise behavior, righteousness, justice and equity.[33] Man is not to live by bread alone but by every word that proceeds out of the mouth of God.[34] In fact, we are told that however a child is trained, that's the way he will go for the rest of his life.[35] This is why Bible-believing Christians are freshly concerned about what's happening in public education.

America's early schools openly taught the role that God and the Bible played in the founding of our nation. But today's textbooks deliberately censor God and the faith of our founding fathers from all mention. A recent study of social study text-

30. C.S. Lewis, *Abolition of Man,* as quoted by Paul C. Vitz in *Censorship: Evidence of Bias in Our Children's Textbooks* (Ann Arbor, MI: Servant Books, 1986), p. 4.

31. Ephesians 6:4.

32. Proverbs 1:7.

33. Proverbs 1:3.

34. Jesus quoted this Old Testament scripture (Deuteronomy 8:3) in Matthew 4:4.

35. Proverbs 22:6.

books shows what has happened. In his informative book *Censorship: Evidence of Bias in our Children's Textbooks,* Dr. Paul C. Vitz writes:

In the first part of the project a total of sixty representative social studies textbooks were carefully evaluated. In grades 1 through 4 these books introduce the child to U.S. society — to family life, community activities, ordinary economic transactions, and some history. None of the books covering grades 1 through 4 contains one word referring to any religious activity in contemporary American life. For example, not one word refers to any child or adult who prayed, or who went to church or temple. The same was true for the twenty grade 5 and 6 texts, as well.

In a very general way the family is often mentioned in the textbooks, but the idea that marriage is the origin and foundation of the family is never presented. Indeed, the words *marriage, wedding, husband, wife,* do not occur once in these books. Nowhere is it suggested that being a mother or homemaker was a worthy and important role for a woman.

High school books covering U.S. history were also studied, and none came close to adequately presenting the major religious events of the past 100 to 200 years. Most disturbing was the constant omission of reference to the large role that religion has always played in American life.

Some particular examples of the bias against religion are significant. One social studies book has thirty pages on the Pilgrims, including the first Thanksgiving. But there is not one word (or image) that referred to religion as even a part of the Pilgrims' life.

Another example is provided by a story of the Nobel laureate and Jewish writer Isaac Bashevis Singer. In his original story the main character, a boy, prayed 'to God' and later remarked 'Thank God.' In the story as presented in the sixth-grade reader the words 'to God' were taken out and the expression 'Thank God' was changed to 'Thank goodness.'[36]

How this nation went from an educational system that recognized and honored God to one that will not even mention His name is a story of intrigue and conspiracy. A detailed account is certainly beyond the scope of this book,[37] but we can look at several highlights. Just how far back does the Christian versus humanist battle for education go?

Robert Owen is called the father of socialism in America. (And no one should forget that socialism is what the communists have always proclaimed as their goal.) Owen came to America in 1825 to set up his utopian commune at a place called New Harmony in Indiana. One of his followers was the influential writer and editor, Orestes Brownson, who later became a Christian and exposed the socialists' scheme to convert America from the worship of God to the worship of the State. Brownson wrote:

> The great object was to get rid of Christianity, and to convert our churches into halls of science. The plan was not to make open attacks on religion although we might belabor the clergy and bring them into contempt where we could; but to establish a system of state — we said national — schools, *from which all religion was to be excluded,* in which nothing was to be taught but such knowledge as is verifiable by the senses and to which all parents were to be compelled by law to send their children....The first thing to be done was to get this system of schools established. For this purpose a secret society was formed....[38] [Italics added.]

At this point in history there were no government schools in America. Children attended private, church and charity schools. In fact, when the plan of establishing common (government) schools was made in Boston in 1817 it was discovered that 96 percent of the town's children were already

---

36. Paul Vitz, op. cit., pp. 1-4.

37. For a thorough treatment of this subject, see *The Messianic Character of American Education* by Rousas John Rushdoony (Nutley, NJ: The Craig Press, 1972).

38. William F. Jasper, *The New American,* September 28, 1986, p. 29.

attending school and the 4 percent who were not had charity schools to attend if the parents wanted to send them. So the idea to start government schools was rejected.[39] But the Socialists never gave up.

It has always been difficult for the American mind to think that any group of persons would conspire to do something as evil as to steer our children from worshiping God to worshiping man. But this is precisely what has happened, and is still happening.

Orestes Brownson exposed the conspiracy in his day:

> To this end it was proposed to organize the whole Union secretly, very much on the plan of Carbonari of Europe, of whom at the time I knew nothing. The members of this secret society were to avail themselves of all the means in their power, each in his own locality, to form public opinion in favor of education by the state at the public expense, and to get such men elected to the legislatures as would be likely to favor our purposes. How far the secret organization extended, I do not know; but I do know that a considerable portion of the State of New York was organized, for I was myself one of the agents for organizing it.[40]

One of the leading education reformers of the 19th Century was the Illinois State Superintendent of Public Instruction, Newton Bateman. Addressing the National Education Association, Bateman prophesied:

> Through costly experiments, splendid failures, and baffled hopes, we make our way toward the Augustan age. As the Israelite awaits the readvent of the lost glory of his race, the Christian the dawn of the millenial day, and the millions the coming of that good time when the earth shall be greener and the skies brighter, so we believe in the golden age of schools and teachers.[41]

Lest you think that Bateman meant no real harm to parental rights, look at this:

39. Ibid.
40. Ibid.
41. William F. Jasper, loc cit., p. 30.

...over all of these minds and souls and bodies, with their untold possibilities of good, the State has, in my opinion, a sort of right of eminent domain and not only may, but should, exercise it in the interest of her own prosperity and dignity.[42]

If you have ever had dealings with government when it claims a right of eminent domain, then you know what Bateman was claiming: that government's right to educate your children with the religion of humanism exceeds your parental right to educate your children with the religion of Christ.

In 1933, John Dewey co-authored *Humanist Manifesto I* calling for the establishment of the religion of humanism. John Dewey is rightly called the father of progressive (modern) education. He sought to convert every government school building into a temple (as Horace Mann called them) for the worship of the godless religion of humanism. John Dewey and modern education have succeeded — except in those wonderfully courageous situations where Christian teachers continue to sift out the socialism and moral anarchy of the humanists and insert the Biblical morality and constitutional principles that marked education during our founding period.

Dewey's humanism has been disastrous for education not only morally, but also academically. How bad has the government school system become?

- Some 23 million adults are functionally illiterate by the simplest tests of everyday reading, writing and comprehension.
- At the end of their grade school education, only three out of five are reading at the skill level appropriate for their age; 84 percent are unable to write an adequate imaginative essay; and 81 percent couldn't produce a simple factual description.
- Scores on the College Board's Scholastic Aptitude Test (SAT) demonstrate a virtually unbroken decline from 1963 to 1980.
- International comparisons of student achievement, completed a decade ago, reveal that on 19 academic

42. Ibid.

36

tests, American students were never first or second; and in comparison with other industrialized nations, were last seven times.[43]

Our public school system is so bad that one of its leading proponents has stated:

American schools are in trouble. In fact, the problems of schooling are of such crippling proportions that many schools may not survive. It is possible that our entire public education system is nearing collapse.[44]

Early Americans did quite well educating their children without government schools. John Adams remarked in 1765: "[A] native of America who cannot read or write is as rare as a comet or an earthquake."[45] In the 1840 census, about 90 percent of white adults were listed as literate.[46]

Let us work and pray for the day when every community offers parents the right to send their children to the school of their choice. The schools should operate somewhat on a free enterprise basis. Let the Christian administrators and teachers raise the funds to purchase a school building and offer basic education under the umbrella of their Christian faith. Let the humanist administrators and teachers raise the funds to purchase a school building and offer progressive education under the umbrella of their worship of man. Then, let the marketplace determine which type of education will succeed and which will fail. And let no one be forced to pay for a type of education he does not want. Which system do you think would soon be the most prevalent where you live?

One of the biggest hurdles you will run into in promoting a plan like this is the National Education Association. Because of this, we need to take a closer look at the NEA.

The National Education Association

At its inception in 1857, the National Education Association was determined to create its own kind of national system of

43. William F. Jasper, loc. cit., pp. 27, 49.

44. Dr. John I. Goodlad, former Dean of UCLA Graduate School of Education as quoted in *The New American,* September 29, 1986, p. 27.

45. *The New American,* September 29. 1986, p. 28.

46. Ibid.

education. Those educators who agreed with the wisdom of America's founders in keeping the federal government out of education were eventually overwhelmed by NEA members, virtually all of whom wanted federal power over the process. Today, the NEA's original goal has been realized.

Undoubtedly, the most famous of NEA leaders was John Dewey. It was this man who, two generations ago, introduced the new techniques to teach reading that have led to widespread illiteracy in America. An admitted socialist, Dewey believed that the greatest enemy of socialism was the private consciousness that could exercise its own judgment. He actually set about to destroy proven educational programs in order to create a more controllable society.

Today, the NEA is the nation's most powerful labor union, and one of the nation's most potent political activist groups. A survey of recent stands taken by the NEA shows that it backs Marxist revolution in Central America; it never criticizes the USSR; it wages incessant propaganda warfare against America's conservatives; it wants all schools and all teachers (not just those in government schools) brought under government control; it is uncompromisingly atheistic; it despises the free enterprise system and loves socialism; and it advocates public, amoral sex education in the schools, abortion on demand, passage of the Equal Rights Amendment, gun control, and disarmament.

For all practical purposes, the NEA might be labeled "the Socialist Party in America." Its program is being given to America's children by many of its teacher members. Christian parents must be made aware of what this organization and its affiliated state agencies are promoting. And all Christians have to be made aware that their taxes are supporting the schools into which the NEA's dangerously un-Christian and un-American agenda is being introduced. Fortunately, not all members of the NEA agree with its positions and goals. Unfortunately, the dues and influences of all the members of the NEA are used to support its positions and goals.

RELIGION

In 1933, the authors of *Humanist Manifesto I* openly sought to establish a new religion which they called religious humanism. But by 1973, the authors of *Humanist Manifesto II* avoided calling their creed a religion and claimed it was simply an ethical process.[47] However, they did admit that humanism is being advanced under many guises:

> Many kinds of humanism exist in the contemporary world. The varieties and emphases of naturalistic humanism include "scientific," "ethical," "democratic," "religious," and "Marxist" humanism. Free thought, atheism, agnosticism, skepticism, deism, rationalism, ethical culture, and liberal religion all claim to be heir to the humanist tradition.[48]

The liberal religion these humanists refer to would certainly include such organizations as the National Council of Churches (NCC). Not all members of those churches belonging to the NCC promote religious humanism. But many ill-informed Christians — while believing their religious leaders can do no wrong - have been lulled to sleep while their offerings and influence are being used to promote religion at war with God, Christianity and America.

National Council of Churches

With the founding of the Federal Council of Churches of Christ in America in 1908, the drive to promote socialism in the churches of America was formally begun. One of the founders of the Federal Council was Dr. Harry F. Ward. An identified communist, Ward also helped found the Communist Party USA in 1919.

In 1935, the Office of Naval Intelligence branded the Federal Council a "radical pacifist organization" that could be counted on to "give aid and comfort to the Communist Party." During the 1940s, the Council fell into disrepute as its parroting of the communist line became obvious. Then in 1950, at a meeting in Cleveland, the Federal Council was reorganized into the National Council of Churches (NCC).

The positions taken by the NCC over the years have remarkably paralleled those taken by the Communist Party. In

47. *Humanist Manifesto I & II,* p. 15.
48. Ibid.

39

1960, a U.S. Air Force Reserve Training Manual warned Air Force personnel that communists and their dupes and sympathizers had infiltrated America's churches. Staff Director Richard Arens of the House Committee on Un-American Activities testified in hearing regarding the charges in the Air Force Manual as follows:

> Thus far of the leadership of the National Council of Churches of Christ in America, we have found over 100 persons in leadership capacity with either Communist-front records or records of service to Communist causes.

Several organizations have published condemnations of the NCC. And a large number of churches have withdrawn from membership in the organization. But its leftwing, socialist and pro-communist leanings continue to have a strong impact on mainline Protestant denominations and their congregations. Many of the members of these churches would be horrified to learn that their offerings to their churches help to finance the National Council of Churches.

Most Americans have difficulty comprehending the idea that someone who does not believe in God could possibly be said to have a religion. But even the United States Supreme Court has referred to humanism as the "religion of secularism."[49]

There can be no doubt that this godless religion understands and has declared war on any religion that believes in God (theism):

> As in 1933, humanists still believe that traditional theism, especially faith in the prayer-hearing God, assumed to love and care for persons, to hear and understand their prayers, and to be able to do something about them, is an unproved and outmoded faith.
>
> Promises of immortal salvation or fear of eternal damnation are both illusory and harmful.
>
> We find insufficient evidence for belief in the existence of a supernatural....
>
> We need, instead, radical new human purposes and goals....

49. John W. Whitehead and John Conlan, "The Establishment of the Religion of Secular Humanism and Its First American Implication," *Texas Tech Law Review*, Vol. X, No. 1 (Lubbock, TX, 1979), pp.20-21.

As non-theists, we begin with humans not God, nature not deity.[50]

I would challenge all ministers in America to stand straight in their pulpits this Sunday morning and clearly state the basis of their ministry. Do you worship God or god? Are you preaching the Bible message of Christianity or the godless religion of humanism? Do you place revealed truth above human reason, or is the Bible at best only man's best ideas about God? Are you leading the sheep in the narrow path of God's Good Shepherd, Jesus, or are you leading them down the popular broad path of humanity leading to destruction?

Church member, how about asking your minister for some clear cut answers (preferably in writing) to these questions? And don't forget to read your Bible regularly. The Bible says the Bereans were noble because they checked the scriptures daily to see if the things being preached to them were true.[51]

We have seen how the humanists have conspired against the family by promoting homosexuality, abortion, government education, and humanistic religion. Now let's look at another vital weapon they use against God, family, and country — socialism.

SOCIALISM

It might be surprising to some that socialism would be listed as a part of the conspiracy against the family. But to anyone who really understands socialism, there should be no surprise at all.

Socialism is a political and economic theory based on collective or governmental control (or outright ownership) and democratic management of the essential means for production and distribution of goods.[52] Socialism is the system Karl Marx proposed in the *Communist Manifesto*. Any free people who follow this socialist plan will find themselves easy picking for a communist takeover. As with the author of the *Humanist Manifesto,* Marx appears to have understood God's revealed principles regarding economics and civil government very well.

50. *Humanist Manifesto I & II,* pp. 13-16.
51. Acts 17:11.
52. *Webster's New Collegiate Dictionary* (Springfield, MA: G. & C. Merriam, 1959).

41

He has thought God's principles through to their direct opposites, and then claimed that putting his principles into practice would bring mankind the greatest possible prosperity and freedom. In reality, it has always done exactly the reverse: it has resulted in the greatest possible prosperity and power for the elite-minded individuals who originally supported socialism for this very purpose.

What are God's and Marx's ideas about economic and governmental systems, anyway? First, let's look at economic systems. Karl Marx and all the communists and socialists would like you to believe that economics gives you only two major choices: capitalism or communism. Capitalism, they tell us, exploits the worker, hurts the poor and helps the rich. Communism, they assure us, treats everyone equally, eliminates poverty, and was even practiced by the early church.

Actually, economics does give you only two major choices: competitive capitalism and monopolistic capitalism. You see, every economic system begins with capital. Even the communists are capitalists. What is capital? Capital is the means of production: tools, factories, farm equipment, etc. The question is not whether or not an economic system will be based on capital. The question is whether capital will be owned privately and competitively or collectively and monopolistically.

Our forefathers chose to allow capital to be owned privately and competitively. That decision led to a great deal of freedom and productivity. But their decision was made after a disastrous first experience. At first, our forefathers did not allow capital to be owned or used privately and competitively. At first, they pooled their capital, everyone worked the same common cornfields, and all shared equally the fruit of everyone's labors. Or should I say, all starved equally on the fruit of their collective labor. That is, until the second planting in 1623 when individual lots were parceled out with the stipulation that the corn grown on these lots would be for the planter's own private use. Here is the first-hand account of what happened when the earliest settlers of Plymouth colony finally switched from monopolistic capitalism to competitive capitalism:

> ...it made all hands very industrious, so as much

42

more corn was planted than otherwise would have been by any means the Governor of any other could use, and saved him a great deal of trouble and gave far better content. The women now went willingly into the field and took their little ones with them to set corn, which before would allege weakness and inability, whom to have compelled would have been thought great tyranny and oppression.[53]

The Pilgrims should have known from their study of the Bible that God's blessings would have been upon a private system rather than a collective system. The early church did not practice communism or monopolistic capitalism or collectivism.

But doesn't the Bible tell us that the early Christians had all things in common? Yes, and we will take a close look at that passage of scripture, but first let's get one thing straight: under monopolistic capitalism, there is either a complete denial of right to own property or, if ownership is allowed, the owner is not allowed to decide how it will be used. Under monopolistic capitalism all property is owned and/or controlled collectively, almost always by government. Anyone operating outside government's control is considered an enemy of the people.

Soon after the start of the church - the Bible says that those early Christians didn't consider their possessions their own but they had all things in common.

There were no needy persons among them. For from time to time those who owned lands or houses sold them, brought the money from the sales and put it at the apostles' feet, and it was distributed to anyone as he had need.[54]

"Wow!" someone exclaims, "The basis for the communist slogan, 'From each according to his ability, to each according to his need' is right here in the Bible." But don't forget that Satan disguises himself as an angel of light. And scripture, like all other writings, must be interpreted in its context.

53. Peter Marshall and David Manuel, *The Light and the Glory* (Old Tappan, NJ: Fleming H. Revell, 1977), p. 141.

54. Acts 4:34, 35.

43

In context, the Bible says those Christians were free to give their possessions if they wanted to do so and they were also free not to give their possessions. The scripture passage involves a couple who devised a plan to deceive the church. They sold their property, held back a part of the proceeds of the sale, and claimed that the smaller amount they were giving to the church was everything they owned. (Possibly their scheme was to make themselves eligible to live off the church for the rest of their lives while secretly hiding a nice little nest egg.) The apostle Peter became aware of the little scheme and addressed its author as follows: "Ananias, how is it that Satan has so filled your heart that you have lied to the Holy Spirit and have kept for yourself some of the money you received for the land? Didn't it belong to you before it was sold? And after it was sold, wasn't the money at your disposal?"[55] The rest of the story isn't very pretty as both Anaias and his wife die when confronted with their deceit. But the point of this scriptural economics lesson is that this couple was free to sell their land or not sell it. Once sold, they were free to give all or none.

Only competitive capitalism allows people the freedom to dispose of their possessions as they choose. By the way, have you noticed that over the past decade or two we are having less and less freedom to dispose of our possessions as we choose? That's because our political leaders have slowly been converting the American system from competitive capitalism to monopolistic capitalism. Ever so gradually, control over our income and property has shifted from ourselves to our government.

The Bible charges individuals, not government, with the responsibility to feed the poor. And it charges governments with the responsibility to protect the rights of the poor (as well as all of us). But have you noticed that our government has gradually taken over the responsibility of caring for the poor, and has instituted programs to confiscate our hard-earned money to do it?

A collectivist government helps the poor differently from how a Bible-believing Christian would. The Christian would see to it that the poor gets the help. The government sees to it

55. Acts 5:3, 4a.

44

that an ever-growing bureaucracy gets the bulk of the help. The Christian would try to help the poor pull up out of his poverty and become self-supporting. Socialist bureaucrats need more poor clamoring for more help in order to justify a larger government that will control more and more of our lives. There are some scoundrels in the community that the Christian would not help, but the government does. In fact, government creates a system where the worst scoundrels get the most assistance. The Christian would give his help in the name of Jesus. The government prevents this in two ways: first, by legally stealing the Christian's abundance through excessive taxation, and second, by making it impossible for any God-believing religion to have an influence in the whole process.

There are many examples in the Bible of God's approval of competitive capitalism. The parables of Jesus always illustrated competitive capitalism at work, not monopolistic capitalism. For example, recall the landowner's response to the salary dispute: "Is it not lawful for me to do what I wish with what is my own? Or, is your eye envious because I am generous?"[56] In the Old Testament we read: "When you shall eat of the labor of your hands, you will be happy and it will be well with you."[57] The most common way the Bible referred to God's approved economic system was this: "...Judah and Israel lived in safety, each man under his own vine and fig tree."[58]

Why does the God of all the universe trouble Himself with concern over such a "trifling" matter as mankind's economic systems? Because God knew before man did that more slavery can be forced upon mankind by government control over property than by all the military wars man ever waged. A good case at hand is what has happened in America over the past 50 years. In order to maintain the same standard of living as their grandparents (with grandpa as wage-earner and grandma as homemaker), today's couple both have to work as wage-earners. The husband to support the family's standard of living and the wife to pay for ever-rising taxes.

Figure it out for yourself. Over 40 percent of the average

56. Matthew 20:15.

57. *New American Standard Bible* (LaHabra, CA: The Lockman Foundation, 1971), Psalm 128:2.

58. I Kings 4:25.

45

worker's gross income goes to pay taxes. Add up all the taxes your family pays in a year: federal, state and local. Don't forget the sales tax, which for a hamburger is now more than the hamburger itself cost a generation ago. Don't forget to add in Social Security tax, income tax, gasoline tax, property tax, the corporation taxes that are always passed on to consumers with higher prices, and scores of other taxes that are making all of us government serfs.

Have you had enough time to add up all your taxes? Okay, now compare that total to how much your wife's take-home pay is. For the average family the amounts are about the same. Which means that most mothers have to labor on behalf of an increasingly socialistic government so the family can barely hang on financially. Socialist bureaucrats will tell you that you are causing your own problems by being so much more materialistic than your grandparents. The truth of the matter is that in 1930 only 5 percent of the Gross National Product (GNP) went to the government. Today, up to 50 percent of the GNP is consumed by government spending.[59] Wild spending is the problem — not on your part, but on your government's part. But that's all part of overthrowing a free people. Unfortunately, it's working.

It is beyond the scope of this little book to deal in depth with the hidden tax called inflation (again something caused by socialism and blamed on the people), or with the causes of the radical booms and busts of the business cycle (caused not by competitive capitalism but by monopolistic capitalism). An excellent book explaining both of these subjects is *The Age of Inflation* (Hans F. Sennholz: Boston, Massachusetts, Western Islands, 1979).

It is also beyond the scope of this book to deal in depth with the subject of the different forms of civil government and how the humanists use socialism to get a free people to give up their freedom. But let's look at this subject briefly.

In the definition of socialism I used the term "democratic." In the *Communist Manifesto* Karl Marx stated, "The first step in the revolution...is to win the battle for democracy." This surprises most people, who say, "Democracy? That's what

59. *The New American,* November 9, 1987, p. 49.

America is, isn't it? At least that's what I learned in government school."

No, our forefathers did not establish a democracy. They established a republic. *"Democracy"* comes from two Greek words: *"demos"* — *"people"* and *"kratein"* — *"to rule;"* i.e., *"the people to rule."*[60] Majority rule. That has a nice ring to it. It sounds fine to an American until he realizes that majority rule leads to mob rule, which is anarchy, and anarchy is a sure route to tyranny.

This is exactly the process Absalom used to overthrow his father, King David. He created dissatisfaction on the part of the people and then promised everything to everybody if they would make him king. He used mob rule to overthrow King David. The people were never quite sure how they ended up living in tyranny. It looked to them as though they had simply gone from having one king to having another. However, they had, in fact, gone from having a *servant* leader to having an *authoritarian* leader.

Bible-believing Christians know the difference between a servant leader and an authoritarian leader because of what Jesus taught in Matthew 20:25-28:

> Jesus called them together and said, "You know that the rulers of the Gentiles lord it over them, and their high officials exercise authority over them. Not so with you. Instead, whoever wants to become great among you must be your servant, and whoever wants to be first must be your slave — just as the Son of Man did not come to be served, but to serve, and to give his life as ransom for many."

George Washington, who said it is impossible to rightly govern the world without God and the Bible, understood this teaching of Jesus very well. The man who refused to be king (authoritarian leader) became instead our nation's President (servant leader) once the proper boundaries were placed on the federal government by the Constitution.

That's what a republic is: a government with definite boundaries upon it to assure that is remains the servant of the peo-

60. John F. McManus, *"An Overview of Our World,"* p.7.

ple, not their master. *"Republic"* comes from two Latin words: *"res"* — *"thing"* and *"publica"* — *"public;"*, i.e., *"the public thing"* — the law — the Constitution.[61] Not only are those who run the civil government to be servant leaders, but they are to be bound down by the chains of public law — a constitution. Thomas Jefferson exhorted his countrymen to "bind men down from mischief by the chains of the Constitution."[62] God gave to Moses for His people as their form of civil government a constitutional republic, a set of rules (laws) which no one, not even a majority of the people or a future king and his government,[63] were to be above.

Some of our forefathers were afraid to establish a federal government over the thirteen independent colonies. They were fearful that it would grow in power and try to exercise the same authority over their lives as had the European governments from which they had fled. However, they were afraid not to establish a federal government because almost any European nation could reconquer a single colony. So, what did they do? They created a federal government v-e-r-y c-a-r-e-f-u-l-l-y. They created a constitutional republic and gave it strictly limited powers so it would remain their servant. They did everything they could to protect themselves from the whims of majorities swayed by demagogues who promise everything to everyone to gain power.

But, a constitutional republic will work only as long as the citizens exercise individual responsibility. A republic is easily set aside (even though the name might still be retained) by anyone who can sway the populace to neglect their heritage of individual responsibility.

Can't you see how important the morality issue is to freedom? Can't you see why those who want America to fall to a world tyranny preach the amorality of the humanists? They can't possibly succeed unless a generation of Americans is per-

61. John F. McManus, loc. cit., p. 8.

62. Ibid.

63. Deuteronomy 17:18-20a - "When he [the King] takes the throne of his kingdom, he is to write for himself on a scroll a copy of this law, taken from that of the priests, who are Levites. It is to be with him, and he is to read it all the days of his life so that he may learn to revere the Lord his God and follow carefully all the words of this law and these decrees and not consider himself better than his brothers and turn from the law to the right or to the left."

suaded to look the other way. The power they could never forcibly take from us is becoming theirs by default. Government power continues to grow while we are busy doing our own thing, elevating pleasure as the greatest good, and excusing ourselves with the attitude that it's all gotten too complicated for the average guy to comprehend, so we'd better leave it up the the "experts."

Even if there had been no evil conspiracy to get us to this point, all that power left lying around would be too tempting for self-promoting individuals not to grasp. If a people refuses to lead itself, it will be led by a totalitarian government. Whether America arrived at its present condition by conspiracy or by default, what we must do is the same. Pick up the power. Take back what's been lost. Simply get back to individual responsibility, to the constitutional republic, and to competitive capitalism. It won't be easy, but it's that simple. This will stop America's downward slide and restore lost freedoms because America will be restored to God's principles of economics and civil government. It's your "valley of decision," America. Choose wisely.

One major tentacle of the conspiracy remains to be dealt with in the next chapter: world government vs. American sovereignty.

"RESOLVED by the American Legion in National Convention...that we demand, once more, that the Congress of the United States launch a comprehensive investigation into the Trilateral Commission and the Council on Foreign Relations to determine what influence has been and is being exerted over the foreign and domestic policies of the United States...."[1]

— 4 —

THE CONSPIRACY AGAINST AMERICAN SOVEREIGNTY

The Council on Foreign Relations (CFR) and the Trilateral Commission (TC) have been heated topics of discussion among political conservatives for years. So, too, has been the conspiratorial view of history. Briefly, let's look at the CFR and the TC: their current influence on America, their beginnings and beliefs, their attitude about American sovereignty, where they are taking America, and what you and I can do about the stranglehold they have on our nation. I have drawn heavily from *The Council on Foreign Relations 1986-1987 ANNUAL REPORT*[2] and from the research contained in *The Insiders* by John F. McManus.[3]

Currently, the membership of the CFR is made up of 2,440 members among whom are 678 business executives (including banking); 608 academic scholars and administrators; 318 U.S. government officials; 292 non-profit institution administrators;

1. Resolution 243 by the American Legion in National Convention assembled in Honolulu, Hawaii, September 1-3, 1981.

2. I secured a copy by writing Council on Foreign Relations, 58 East 68th Street, New York, NY 10021.

3. John F. McManus, *The Insiders* (Belmont, MA: The John Birch Society, 1983). An information packet including this book is available for $3 from American Opinion, 395 Concord Ave., Belmont, MA 02178 or American Opinion, 2650 Mission St., San Marino, CA 91108. All material used with permission of the author.

262 journalists, correspondents and communications executives; 129 lawyers; and 43 others.[4]

The business executives include:

Donald M. Kendall	Chairman	PepsiCo., Inc.
Thomas V. Jones	Chairman	Northrop Corporation
Ruben F. Mettler	Chairman	TRW, Inc.
Roberto C. Goizueta	Chairman	The Coca-Cola Co.
Willard C. Butcher	Chairman	Chase Manhattan Bank
Dwayne O. Andreas	Chairman	Ancher Daniels Midland Co.
James E. Burke	Chairman	Johnson & Johnson
Robert A. Hanson	Chairman	Deere & Company
Alan Greenspan	Chairman	Federal Reserve System
Ralph A. Pfeiffer, Jr.	Chairman	IBM World Trade
John F. Welch, Jr.	Chairman	General Electric Co.
Robert Anderson	Chairman	Rockwell International
Clifton C. Garvin	Chairman	Exxon Corporation
Donald E. Peterson	Chairman	Ford Motor Company
David T. Kearns	Chairman	Xerox Corporation
Alexander B. Trowbridge	President	Nat'l. Assn. of Manufacturers

The government officials include:

George C. Schultz	Secretary of State
Frank C. Carlucci	Secretary of Defense
Colin L. Powell	National Security Advisor
C. William Verity	Secretary of Commerce
Howard H. Baker	White House Chief of Staff
William H. Webster	Directer, CIA
John C. Whitehead	Deputy Secretary of State
Jack F. Matlock, Jr.	Ambassador to USSR
Winston Lord	Ambassador to the People's Republic of (Communist) China
Max M. Kampelman	State Department Arms Negotiator
Michael H. Armacost	Under-Secretary of State for Political Affairs

U.S. Senators:

Rudy Boschwitz	Minnesota
John H. Chafee	Rhode Island
William S. Cohen	Maine
Christopher J. Dodd	Connecticut
Bob Graham	Florida
Daniel P. Moynihan	New York
Claiborne Pell	Rhode Island
Larry Pressler	South Dakota

4. Kempton Dunn, Director of Membership Affairs, "Membership," *Council on Foreign Relations ANNUAL REPORT,* July 1, 1986-June 30, 1987 (New York, NY: Council on Foreign Relations, 1987), p. 86.

John D. Rockefeller, IV	West Virginia
William V. Roth, Jr.	Delaware
Warren B. Rudman	New Hampshire
Terry Sanford	North Carolina
Lowell P. Weicker	Connecticut
Timothy E. Wirth	Colorado

The journalists, correspondents and communications executives include:

Media Executives:

Thornton F. Bradshaw	Chairman	RCA Corp. (NBC)
Roone Arledge	President	ABC News
William S. Paley	Chairman	CBS
Henry Muller	Managing Editor	*Time*
Richard M. Smith	Editor-in-Chief	*Newsweek*
Peter W. Bernstein	Managing Editor	*US News & World Report*
Max Frankel	Executive Editor	*New York Times*
Katharine Graham	Chairman	*Washington Post*
W. Thomas Johnson	Publisher	*Los Angeles Times*

Print Journalists:

James Reston	Joseph C. Harsch
George Will	William F. Buckley, Jr.
Flora Lewis	Marquis Childs
Hodding Carter, III	

Radio/TV Journalists:

David Brinkley	John Chancellor
Charles Collingwood	Richard C. Hottelet
Dan Rather	Daniel L. Schorr
Jim Lehrer	Robert L. McNeill
Barbara Walters	Irving R. Levine[5]

The Trilateral Commission membership presently includes approximately 90 North Americans, 90 Western Europeans, and 75 Japanese.

Among the current Trilateralists can be found:

Henry A. Kissinger	Former Secretary of State
David Rockefeller	Former Chairman of Chase Manhattan Bank
John H. Glenn, Jr.	U.S. Senator (Ohio)
Jeane J. Kirkpatrick	Former Ambassador to the U.N.
Lane Kirkland	President of AFL/CIO
David Stockman	Former Director of Office of Management and Budget

5. "Membership Roster, June 30, 1987," *Council on Foreign Relations ANNUAL REPORT,* op. cit., pp. 132-148.

| Robert S. McNamara | Former Secretary of Defense |
| Zbigniew Brzezinski | Former National Security Advisor |

Former members of the TC currently in government service include:

George Bush	Vice President
William E. Brock	Secretary of Labor
Frank C. Carlucci	Secretary of Defense
Winston Lord	U.S. Ambassador to the People's Republic of China

TC alumni include:

Caspar W. Weinberger	Former Secretary of Defense
Walter F. Mondale	Former Minnesota U.S. Senator and Presidential Candidate
Paul A. Volcker	Former Chairman, Federal Reserve Board
Barber B. Conable, Jr.	President, World Bank
Jimmy Carter	Former U.S. President[6]

I think you will agree that the members of these two organizations wield a great deal of influence on America. The CFR is a privately funded council whose stated purpose is to study the international aspects of American political, economic, and strategic problems. The TC purposes include linking North America, Western Europe, and Japan in their economic relations, their political and defense relations, their relations with developing countries, and their relations with Communist countries.

All of this sounds pretty bland and of little interest to the average citizen. However, a brief review of the beginnings of these internationalist-minded organizations is guaranteed to raise more than a few eyebrows. If the full story about these groups becomes known by Americans soon enough, the public's increasing level of concern about what's happening to our great land can be channeled into informed and concerted action that can steer us back to individual responsibility, free us from strangling collectivism, and restore our national sovereignty.

The Council on Foreign Relations incorporated in 1921....[7] The CFR's founder, Edward Mandell

6. Trilateral Commission, 345 E. 46th Street, New York, NY 10017.
7. Dan Smoot, *The Invisible Government,* (Boston, MA: Western Islands, 1977).

House, had been the chief advisor of President Woodrow Wilson. House dominated the President. Woodrow Wilson referred to House as "my alter ego" (my other self), and it is totally accurate to say that House, not Wilson, was the most powerful individual in our nation during the Wilson Administration, from 1913 until 1921.

Unfortunately for America, it is also true that Edward Mandell House was a Marxist whose goal was to socialize the United States. In 1912, House wrote the book, *Philip Dru: Administrator*.[8] In it, he said he was working for Socialism as dreamed of by Karl Marx....

In *Philip Dru: Administrator*.... House laid out a fictionalized plan for the conquest of America. He told of a "conspiracy" (the word is his) which would gain control of both the Democratic and Republican Parties, and use them as instruments in the creation of a socialistic world government.

The book called for passage of a graduated income tax and for the establishment of a state-controlled central bank as steps toward the ultimate goal. Both of these proposals are planks in the *Communist Manifesto*. And both became law in 1913, during the very first year of the House-dominated Wilson Administration.

The House plan called for the United States to give up its sovereignty to the League of Nations at the close of World War I. But when the U.S. Senate refused to ratify America's entry into the League, Edward Mandell House's drive toward world government was slowed down. Disappointed, but not beaten, House and his friends then formed the Council of Foreign Relations, whose purpose right from its inception was to destroy the freedom and independence of the United States and lead our nation into a world government — if not through the League of Nations, then through another world

8. Edward Mandell House, *Philip Dru: Administrator,* (New York, NY: 1912).

54

organization that would be started after another world war. The control of that world government, of course, was to be in the hands of House and like-minded individuals.

From its beginning in 1921, the CFR individuals attracted men of power and influence. In the late 1920s important financing for the CFR came from the Rockefeller Foundation and the Carnegie Foundation. In 1940, at the invitation of President Roosevelt, members of the CFR gained domination over the State Department, and they have maintained that domination ever since.

By 1944, Edward Mandell House was deceased, but his plan for taking control of our nation's major political parties began to be realized. In 1944 and in 1948, the Republican candidate for President, Thomas Dewey, was a CFR member. In later years, the CFR could boast that Republicans Eisenhower and Nixon were members, as were Democrats Stevenson, Kennedy, Humphrey, and McGovern. The American people were told they had a choice when they voted for President. But with precious few exceptions, Presidential candidates for decades have been CFR members.[9]

The Trilateral Commission was founded much more recently.

The Trilateral Commission's roots stem from the book *Between Two Ages*,[10] written by Zbigniew Brzezinski in 1970. The following quotations from that book show how closely Brzezinski's thinking parallels that of CFR founder Edward Mandell House.

On page 72, Brzezinski writes: "Marxism is simultaneously a victory of the external, active man over the inner, passive man and a victory of reason over belief."

On page 83, he states: "Marxism, disseminated on the popular level in the form of communism,

9. John F. McManus, op. cit., pp. 6-8.

10. Zbigniew Brzezinski, *Between Two Ages* (New York, NY: Viking Press, 1970 & New York, NY: Penguin Books, 1976).

represented a major advance in man's ability to conceptualize his relationship to his world."

And on page 123, we find: "Marxism supplied the best available insight into contemporary reality."

Nowhere does Mr. Brzezinski tell his readers that the Marxism "in the form of communism" which he praises has been responsible for the murder of approximately 100 million human beings in the Twentieth Century, has brought about the enslavement of over a billion more, and has caused want, privation and despair for all but the few criminals who run the communist-dominated nations.

On page 198, after discussing America's shortcomings, Brzezinski writes: "America is undergoing a new revolution" which "unmasks its obsolescence." We disagree; America is not becoming obsolete.

On page 260, he proposed "Deliberate management of the American future...with the...planner as the key social legislator and manipulator." The central planning that he wants for our country is a cardinal underpinning of communism and the very opposite of the way things are done in a free country....

Brzezinski then calls for the forging of community links among the United States, Western Europe, and Japan; and the extension of these links to more advanced communist countries. Finally, on page 309 of his 309-page book, he lets us know that what he really wants is "the goal of world government."

Zbigniew Brzezinski's *Between Two Ages* was published in 1970 while he was a professor in New York City. What happened, quite simply, is that David Rockefeller read the book. And, in 1973, Mr. Rockefeller launched the new Trilateral Commission, the purposes of which include linking North America, Western Europe, and Japan....

The original literature of the Trilateral Commission also states, exactly as Brzezinski's book had proposed, that the more advanced communist states could become partners in the alliance leading to world government. In short, David Rockefeller implemented Brzezinski's proposal....

Then David Rockefeller hired Zbigniew Brzezinski away from Columbia University and appointed him to be the Director of the Trilateral Commission. Later, in 1973, the little known former governor of Georgia, Jimmy Carter, was invited to become a founding member of the Trilateral Commission. Mr. Carter was later to say: *"Membership on this Commission has provided me with a splendid learning opportunity, and many of the members have helped me in my study of foreign affairs."*[11][12]

Now you have a solid clue as to why the Carter Administration undermined America's friends (the Shah of Iran and Somoza in Nicaragua), gave the back of its hand to anti-communist nations such as South Korea, Taiwan, and Chile, and continued to build up Communist Russia and Communist China.

Marxist conspirators have been running most of the Administrative branch of our government for the past 40 years, including an absolute stranglehold on the State Department (the past ten Secretaries of State dating back to the 1940s have been members of the CFR). So what? What's the big deal? What harm can a one-world Secretary of State do to American sovereignty? With almost 40 continuous years of domination over our State Department, just how much could the Council on Foreign Relations achieve toward its goal of preparing America and the world for a one-world socialist system? Are they willing to start and wage no-win wars and use our sons as just so many pawns on a giant political chessboard? Are they so devious that they can supply so much aid and trade (most of it on credit) that our enemies would collapse without their help? Would they purposely betray entire nations to the communists? Do they take advantage of nations that gullibly follow our State Department's lead, believing all Americans to be anti-communist? What madness would this be? Are these

11. Jimmy Carter, *Why Not the Best?* (Nashville, TN: Broadman Press, 1975.

12. John F. McManus, op. cit., pp. 12-14.

the people the Scriptures tell us can't sleep unless they have done something evil, actually delight in doing evil, and devise it continually?

Here are the Ten, the year they took office and one major action taken by each during his tenure as Secretary of State to further the goals of the Council on Foreign Relations:

George P. Shultz - 1982 - Defused American outrage over the shooting down of KAL 007 by the Soviets.

Alexander M. Haig - 1981 - Arranged first arms sales to Red China.

Edmund S. Muskie - 1980 - Stumped hard for ratification of SALT II.

Cyrus R. Vance - 1977 - Delivered Nicaragua to Reds; also the Panama Canal.

Henry A. Kissinger - 1973 - Delivered Southeast Asia to the communists.

William P. Rogers - 1969 - Betrayed Rhodesia.

Dean Rusk - 1961 - Set the no-win rules in Vietnam.

John Foster Dulles - 1953 - Betrayed Hungarian Freedom Fighters.

Dean Acheson - 1949 - Delivered China to Mao Tse Tung.

Perhaps by now, you are about ready to slam this book against the wall and stomp around the room muttering, "Stop the world and let me off!" European Marxists of the Nineteenth Century drew up a plan to sucker a free people into willingly enslaving themselves, and American Marxists of the Twentieth Century are carrying out that plan on the freest people the world has ever known. Their goal: world domination. Their plan: socialism. Their methods: wolves in sheep's clothing. Their Achilles' heel: your awareness and action.

Let's take a look at what can be done.

"There are those who assess our situation and conclude that all is lost. They say: 'No nation has ever gone as far into collectivism as we in the United States already are, and yet recovered.' Surprisingly, they're right....But there is something that these prophets of doom do not add to their evaluation...no one has ever really tried to reverse the collectivist drive...who's to say that we can't be the first?"

John F. McManus[1]

— 5 —

BUT I'M ONLY ONE PERSON

I make my living as a marriage and family counselor. I have to admit that I take a somewhat professional interest in people who think that they are more than one person, and in people who complain that they are only one person.

Of course, you are only one person. But falling back on that is the poorest excuse in the world for not doing something about a serious problem. What we really mean when we say, "I'm only one person" is "I'm not significant enough." When God called on Moses to lead the children of Israel out of Egypt, Moses made five excuses: 1) I'm a nobody; 2) What authority do I have?; 3) What if they don't believe me?; 4) I'm not a good speaker; 5) Somebody else could do better.[2]

First, nobody is a nobody, especially in America. Second, you have the authority and the responsibility as an American citizen to educate yourself and your neighbors and to vote as your conscience dictates. Third, stand by the truth even if you stand alone. Be true to yourself and to God. Fourth, let the information you give speak for you. Use printed material and videotapes to educate someone else who is a good speaker and an opinion molder. Fifth, there are some people only you can

1. John F. McManus, *"An Overview of Our World,"* the text of a filmstrip produced by The John Birch Society, Belmont, MA, 1971, p. 56.

2. Exodus 3 & 4.

reach. God can only use those who make themselves available. But, oh how He can use a seemingly insignificant person. How about the little boy with five loaves and two fishes?[3] How about a simple fisherman named Peter? How about our self-deprecating Moses? How about that one person God couldn't find to stand in the gap for Jerusalem? You shouldn't be saying, "I'm only one." You should be saying, "I am one."

Who can blame us for feeling like a little David on a battlefield with a giant Goliath? How can one person stand up against a conspiracy involving the people who dominate America's media, the academic world, top corporations, the huge foundations, labor unions, the military, American politics, and just about every other segment of American life? After all, if we focus completely on how gigantic and how entrenched this humanist conspiracy is, we could easily be overwhelmed with despair.

How can we avoid despair? By focusing more on what's right and good rather than on what's wrong and evil. Focus on your family, your heritage, and the things you can do rather than what you've been told one person can't do. Be like the bumble bee who doesn't know that, aerodynamically, he isn't supposed to be able to fly. Act in faith believing that there are others like you all across America who have not "bowed the knee to Baal."[4] "Let us fix our eyes on Jesus"[5] to get things back in perspective.

God is still on His throne but the conspirators are sitting on a house of cards, fearful that more Americans will realize their vulnerability and start kicking at their foundations. Don't forget, our battle is not with flesh and blood. The Satanic conspiracy against everything worthwhile in America would not stop if the CFR and TC ceased suddenly to exist. This is not a conspiracy like the control a puppeteer has over his puppets. Nobody orders these prominent men to promote collectivism

3. John 6:5-14.

4. 1 Kings 19:18.

5. Hebrews 12:2,3 - "Let us fix our eyes on Jesus, the author and perfecter of our faith, who for the joy set before him endured the cross, scorning its shame, and sat down at the right hand of the throne of God. Consider him who endured such opposition from sinful men, so that you will not grow weary and lose heart."

and amorality. These leaders in their various fields are either philosophically committed to the establishment of a new world order or, if they are not, they have found that associating with those who are committed has brought greater personal benefits than they ever thought possible. Not every member of the CFR and TC is fully committed to carrying out House's and Brzezinski's plans to accomplish Marxist goals. But all CFR and TC members are allowing their names and influence to be used by the planners.

When enough people know what you now know, many who previously associated with the CFR and TC will quickly withdraw, claiming not to have known what they were really doing. Remember, "we the people" are the ones all of these leaders depend on to pay the taxes, provide the products and services, buy and consume their goods, watch their TV networks, read their newpapers and magazines, support their universities with our money and our children, and vote them into or out of office.

Doesn't all this suggest the most logical way to fight these principalities, powers, and this spiritual wickedness in high places? First, we have to educate ourselves. Second, we have to exercise individual responsibility and stop doing anything that supports their evil schemes.

Without being a prophet or the son of a prophet, I can predict with absolute certainty how this battle for individualism and morality will come out in Washington. IF WE WIN THE BATTLE IN THE MINDS OF OUR NEIGHBORS, WE WILL WIN THE BATTLE IN WASHINGTON. IF WE DON'T WIN THE BATTLE IN THE MINDS OF OUR NEIGHBORS, WE WILL LOSE THE BATTLE FOR FREEDOM IN WASHINGTON. It's that simple. It won't be easy to win the battle in the minds of our neighbors, but it's that simple.

I believe that, with God's help, three hundred educational warriors (somewhat of a Gideon's army) in every congressional district can turn the tide of the battle. Everyone has a direct influence on at least ten others (300 × 10 = 3,000) and through them an indirect influence upon one hundred (300 × 100 = 30,000).

When 300 humble and courageous citizens (men, women,

and teenagers) become educated, dedicated, and active in every congressional district in America, the humanist conspirators' house of cards will begin to shake.

When 3,000 join the battle, their house of cards will begin to sway.

When 30,000 men, women, and teenagers in every one of the 435 congressional districts in these United States know clearly what they stand for, know clearly what they are against (and how to identify humanist politicians, broadcasters, and educators), and act accordingly, the house of cards will fall. Satan will have to regroup and wait for another generation of Americans to succumb to his plans for world government.

You obviously can't depend on ABC, CBS, or NBC to tell you accurately and openly about the battle between Americanism and Marxist Humanism. We will have to distribute our information through a self-made grassroots educational system. Chapter 6 tells you about some of the people and organizations already waging a part of this battle for a free future. Chapter 7 indexes the voting record of every member of the U.S. Senate and the U.S. House of Representatives so that you can see for yourself whether your Congressman and two Senators are a part of the problem, or a part of the solution.

*"Oh! thus be it ever, when freemen shall stand
Between their loved home, and the war's desolation!
    Blest with victory and peace,
    may the heav'n-rescued land
Praise the Power that hath made and preserved
    us a nation....*

The Star-Spangled Banner (1814)
— Francis Scott Key

— 6 —

FREEDOM'S FRIENDS

Here is a listing of people, publications and organizations promoting morality and individualism and opposing amorality and collectivism. Every Bible-believing Christian should be involved in two or three of these patriotic projects.

The New American magazine is a conservative, bi-weekly journal of news and commentary that offers common-sense perspective and traditional values. Recommended for those sick of writers who weave humanism, relativism, and global ideology into their "news" articles. Best source for keeping up with your Congressman's voting record. ($39.00 per year.) Send to: *The New American,* 395 Concord Avenue, Belmont, MA 02178; (617) 489-0605.

The 700 Club is a daily television program founded by Pat Robertson and seen each week by an estimated 7.2 million viewers. Here is a good source for daily TV news minus the left-wing bias. Produced by Christian Broadcasting Network, Satellite Center, Virginia Beach, VA 23463.

Point of View is a radio show hosted by Marlin Maddoux. Heard via satellite over 200 stations five days per week. Produced by International Christian Media, P.O. Box 30, Dallas, TX 75221: (214) 484-2020.

The John Birch Society is a nationwide educational network whose motto is "Less government, more responsibility, and —

with God's help — a better world.'' For complete information packet that includes — *The Insiders* by John F. McManus, send $3.00 to: The John Birch Society, Belmont, MA 02178; (617) 489-0600.

The Mel Gablers' Newsletter is published by Mr. and Mrs. Mel Gabler, who have spent many years critiquing textbooks used in American schools. Contact them at Educational Research Analysts, P.O. Box 7518, Longview, TX 75607; (214) 753-5993.

Focus on the Family is a film-producing and publishing ministry. Publishes *Focus on the Family* magazine. ($15.00 per year.) *Focus on the Family*, Pomona, CA 91799; (714) 620-8500.

Eagle Forum is an educational and political action group founded by Mrs. Phyllis Schlafly. Publishes *The Phyllis Schlafly Report* monthly. ($15.00 per year.) P.O. Box 618, Alton, IL 62002.

Concerned Women for America is a nationwide prayer and action organization founded by Beverly LaHaye. Publishes *Concerned Women for America News* each month. ($15.00 per year.) 122 "C" Street NW, Suite 800, Washington, D.C. 20001; (202) 628-3014.

The Larry McDonald Crusade to Stop Financing Communism is a network of local committees fighting the giveaways to Socialist and Communist dictatorships. Publishes votes of congressmen and senators on issues involving Communism in its *Crusade Bulletin*. 2650 Mission Street, San Marino, CA 91108; (818) 799-0876.

Tax Reform IMmediately (TRIM) is a network of local committees providing information to Americans about taxes, inflation, and government regulation. Publishes votes of congressmen on issues related to federal spending in its *TRIM Bulletin*. 4 Hill Road, Belmont, MA 02178; (617) 489-0600.

Intercessors For America is a prayer and action group. Publishes the *IFA Newsletter* and provides it upon request. P.O. Box 2639, Reston, VA 22090; (703) 471-0913.

"It is not enough to know what a Congressman says; it is also important to know what he does."

BRI Directory of the 100th Congress

— 7 —

CONGRESS IS THE KEY

While it is important who sits in the White House and what his views are regarding the battle between Christian principles and humanist tenets, the truth is that no matter who is President, he cannot succeed unless a majority of Congress is on the same track. For instance, do you realize the President cannot spend a penny that Congress has not authorized?

Congress is the key to helping our President turn the United States government back to following a course of individualism and morality. But you have to know how your Congressman is voting on the issues. The following voting index is used with permission of Birch Research Incorporated (BRI) and is drawn from the *BRI Directory of the 100th Congress.*[1]

The following index measures a Congressman's overall voting performance dating back to the 96th Congress (1979-1980) depending upon when he entered office. If he entered the House of Representatives in 1979 or before, his percentage includes 1,132 votes. If he entered the Senate in 1979 or before, his percentage covers 959 votes. These votes include the following issues: abortion, agriculture, commerce and transportation, defense and disarmament, economic affairs (appropriations, budget, national debt, taxes), education, energy, environment, foreign affairs, governmental, health and human services, housing and urban development, labor, law and the judiciary, social security.

---

1. *BRI Directory Of The 100th Congress* (Belmont, MA: Birch Research Incorporated, 1987). Available for $4 (including postage and handling charges) from BRI, 395 Concord Ave., Belmont, MA 02178. The BRI Directory breaks down each Congressman's vote by issue and by term of office. It gives detailed instruction for influencing your Congressman between elections including their address and phone numbers and committee assignments.

A high score indicates that a Congressman has voted consistently for competitive capitalism, morality, and American sovereignty. A low vote indicates that a Congressman has voted consistently for Marxist, monopolistic capitalism, humanistic amorality, and internationalism over sovereignty. Are your Representative and two Senators a part of America's problem, or a part of her solution?

Those names printed in *italics* indicate Republican Representatives and Senators.

The House of Representatives[2]

ALABAMA

%

1 *H.L. "Sonny" Callahan*	78
2 *William L. Dickinson*	73
3 Bill Nichols	57
4 Tom Bevill	43
5 Ronnie G. Flippo	42
6 Ben Erdreich	43
7 Claude Harris	52

ALASKA

AL *Don Young*	62

ARIZONA

1 *John Rhodes III*	66
2 Morris K. Udall	16
3 *Bob Stump*	92
4 *Jon Kyl*	87
5 *Jim Kolbe*	78

ARKANSAS

1 Bill Alexander	22
2 Tommy Robinson	52
3 *John P. Hammerschmidt*	69
4 Beryl Anthony, Jr.	29

CALIFORNIA

1 Douglas H. Bosco	23
2 *Wally Herger*	86
3 Robert T. Matsui	14
4 Vic Fazio	16
5 Nancy Pelosi	5

%

6 Barbara Boxer	11
7 George Miller	15
8 Ronald V. Dellums	12
9 Fortney H. "Pete" Stark	12
10 Don Edwards	9
11 Tom Lantos	20
12 *Ernest L. Konnyu*	18
13 Norman Y. Mineta	14
14 *Norman D. Shumway*	91
15 Tony Coelho	18
16 Leon E. Panetta	22
17 *Charles Pashayan, Jr.*	70
18 Richard H. Lehman	14
19 *Robert J. Lagomarsino*	79
20 *William M. Thomas*	75
21 *Elton Gallegly*	85
22 *Carlos J. Moorhead*	86
23 Anthony C. Beilenson	13
24 Henry A. Waxman	13
25 Edward R. Roybal	11
26 Howard L. Berman	8
27 Mel Levine	11
28 Julian C. Dixon	10
29 Augustus F. Hawkins	11
30 Matthew G. Martinez	17
31 Mervyn M. Dymally	10
32 Glenn M. Anderson	31

2. All of the U.S. House of Representative seats are up for election every even-numbered year.

66

	%
33 *David Dreier*	91
34 Esteban Edward Torres	10
35 *Jerry Lewis*	73
36 George E. Brown, Jr	13
37 *Al McCandless*	84
38 *Robert K. Dornan*	80
39 *William E. Dannemeyer*	92
40 *Robert E. Badham*	85
41 *Bill Lowery*	72
42 *Dan Lungren*	88
43 *Ron Packard*	80
44 Jim Bates	22
45 *Duncan L. Hunter*	78

COLORADO

1 Patricia Schroeder	30
2 David E. Skaggs	18
3 *Ben Campbell*	35
4 *Hank Brown*	79
5 *Joel Hefley*	87
6 *Daniel L. Schaefer*	82

CONNECTICUT

1 Barbara B. Kennelly	15
2 Sam Gejdenson	13
3 Bruce A. Morrison	15
4 *Christopher Shays*	50
5 *John G. Rowland*	61
6 *Nancy L. Johnson*	42

DELAWARE

AL Thomas R. Carper	29

FLORIDA

1 Earl Hutto	53
2 Bill Grant	31
3 Charles E. Bennett	43
4 Bill Chappell, Jr	49
5 *Bill McCollum*	78
6 Buddy MacKay	31
7 Sam Gibbons	35
8 *C.W. "Bill" Young*	72
9 *Michael Bilirakis*	78
10 *Andy Ireland*	69
11 Bill Nelson	48
12 *Tom Lewis*	70
13 *Connie Mack*	87

	%
14 Daniel A. Mica	33
15 *E. Clay Shaw, Jr.*	75
16 Larry Smith	16
17 William Lehman	10
18 Claude Pepper	18
19 Dante B. Fascell	17

GEORGIA

1 Robert Lindsay Thomas	36
2 Charles Hatcher	36
3 Richard Ray	54
4 *Patrick L. Swindall*	85
5 John Lewis	9
6 *Newt Gingrich*	75
7 George W. Darden	44
8 J. Roy Rowland	36
9 Ed Jenkins	46
10 Doug Barnard, Jr.	54

HAWAII

1 Patricia Saiki	65
2 Daniel K. Akaka	18

IDAHO

1 *Larry E. Craig*	85
2 Richard Stallings	41

ILLINOIS

1 Charles A. Hayes	8
2 Gus Savage	12
3 Marty Russo	31
4 *Jack Davis*	78
5 William O. Lipinski	32
6 *Henry J. Hyde*	68
7 Cardiss Collins	10
8 Dan Rostenkowski	20
9 Sidney R. Yates	9
10 *John Edward Porter*	59
11 Frank Annunzio	19
12 *Philip M. Crane*	96
13 *Harris W. Fawell*	72
14 *Dennis Hastert*	83
15 *Edward R. Madigan*	62
16 *Lynn Martin*	71
17 Lane Evans	11
18 *Robert H. Michel*	71
19 Terry L. Bruce	16

20 Dick Durbin 18
21 Melvin Price 23
22 Kenneth J. Gray.............17

INDIANA

1 Peter J. Visclosky 16
2 Philip R. Sharp..............32
3 *John Hiler*....................80
4 *Dan Coats*....................74
5 *Jim Jontz*.....................16
6 *Dan Burton* 87
7 *John T. Myers*...............70
8 Frank McCloskey...........20
9 Lee H. Hamilton.............29
10 Andrew Jacobs, Jr..........39

IOWA

1 *Jim Leach*....................42
2 *Tom Tauke* 59
3 *David Nagle* 14
4 Neal Smith 22
5 *Jim Ross Lightfoot* 73
6 Fred Grandy 67

KANSAS

1 *Pat Roberts* 73
2 Jim Slattery 39
3 *Jan Meyers*...................63
4 Dan Glickman...............32
5 *Bob Whittaker* 72

KENTUCKY

1 Carroll Hubbard, Jr. 59
2 William H. Natcher 29
3 Romano L. Mazzoli 30
4 *Jim Bunning* 85
5 *Harold Rogers*...............64
6 *Larry J. Hopkins* 71
7 Carl C. "Chris" Perkins...22

LOUISIANA

1 *Bob Livingston*..............72
2 Lindy (Mrs. Hale) Boggs ..21
3 W.J. "Billy" Tauzin 52
4 Buddy Roemer 65
5 Jerry Huckaby 51
6 *Richard Baker*...............80
7 James A. Hayes 35
8 Clyde Holloway.............80

MAINE

1 *Joseph E. Brennan*..........17
2 *Olympia J. Snowe* 43

MARYLAND

1 Roy Dyson 45
2 *Helen Delich Bentley* 63
3 Benjamin L. Cardin 13
4 *Thomas McMillen* 28
5 Steny H. Hoyer 15
6 Beverly B. Byron............53
7 Kweisi Mfume...............10
8 Constance A. Morella......30

MASSACHUSETTS

1 *Silvio O. Conte*...............25
2 Edward P. Boland 18
3 Joseph D. Early 22
4 Barney Frank 14
5 Chester G. Atkins...........12
6 Nicholas Mavroules 18
7 Edward J. Markey..........13
8 Joseph P. Kennedy II 13
9 Joe Moakley 15
10 Gerry E. Studds 11
11 Brian J. Donnelly 23

MICHIGAN

1 John Conyers, Jr.............14
2 *Carl D. Pursell* 46
3 Howard Wolpe..............14
4 *Frederick S. Upton* 78
5 *Paul B. Henry* 58
6 Bob Carr 22
7 Dale E. Kildee 14
8 Bob Traxler 21
9 *Guy Vander Jagt*............66
10 *Bill Schuette* 66
11 *Robert W. Davis*............51
12 David E. Bonior.............12
13 George W. Crockette, Jr...11
14 Dennis M. Hertel 25
15 William D. Ford 13
16 John D. Dingell 16

17 Sander M. Levin 12
18 *William S. Broomfield* 69

MINNESOTA

1 Timothy J. Penny...........35
2 *Vin Weber* 74
3 *Bill Frenzel*...................65
4 Bruce F. Vento 12
5 Martin Olav Sabo...........10
6 Gerry Sikorski...............15
7 *Arlan Strangeland* 69
8 James L. Oberstar 12

MISSISSIPPI

1 Jamie L. Whitten 24
2 *Mike Espy*...................17
3 G.V. Montgomery..........66
4 Wayne Dowdy 33
5 *Trent Lott*...................77

MISSOURI

1 William Clay.................10
2 Jack Buechner...............77
3 Richard A. Gephardt.......23
4 Ike Skelton...................43
5 Alan Wheat 9
6 *E. Thomas Coleman* 65
7 *Gene Taylor* 77
8 *Bill Emerson*................69
9 Harold L. Volkmer.........37

MONTANA

1 Pat Williams.................19
2 *Ron Marlenee* 76

NEBRASKA

1 *Douglas K. Bereuter*........58
2 *Hal Daub*.....................75
3 *Virginia Smith*..............65

NEVADA

1 James H. Bilbray 33
2 *Barbara F. Vucanovich* 79

NEW HAMPSHIRE

1 *Robert C. Smith*.............90
2 *Judd Gregg* 78

NEW JERSEY

1 James J. Florio..............20
2 William J. Hughes..........36
3 James J. Howard 14
4 *Christopher H. Smith* 36
5 *Marge Roukema* 50
6 Bernard J. Dwyer...........16
7 *Matthew J. Rinaldo* 44
8 Robert A. Roe...............22
9 Robert G. Torricelli 18
10 Peter W. Rodino, Jr....10
11 *Dean A. Gallo*...............65
12 *Jim Courter*...................65
13 *H. James Saxton*............64
14 Frank J. Guarini 18

NEW MEXICO

1 *Manuel Lujan, Jr.* 73
2 *Joe Skeen* 73
3 Bill Richardson..............22

NEW YORK

1 *George Hochbrueckner*....15
2 Thomas J. Downey.........13
3 Robert J. Mrazek 15
4 *Norman F. Lent*.............59
5 *Raymond J. McGrath*......61
6 Floyd H. Flake 15
7 Gary L. Ackerman...........9
8 James H. Scheuer...........12
9 Thomas J. Manton 14
10 Charles E. Schumer 14
11 Edolphus Towns 8
12 Major R. Owens..............9
13 Stephen J. Solarz...........11
14 *Guy V. Molinari* 60
15 *Bill Green* 26
16 Charles B. Rangel 8
17 Ted Weiss 13
18 Robert Garcia..................9
19 Mario Biaggi.................22
20 *Joseph D. DioGuardi* 63
21 *Hamilton Fish, Jr.* 37
22 *Benjamin A. Gilman* 40
23 Samuel S. Stratton..........41
24 *Gerald B.H. Solomon*......83

	%
2 *Floyd Spence*	76
3 Butler Derrick	28
4 *Elizabeth J. Patterson*	38
5 John M. Spratt, Jr.	27
6 Robin Tallon	37

SOUTH DAKOTA

AL Timothy P. Johnson 24

TENNESSEE

1 *James H. Quillen*	65
2 *John J. Duncan*	63
3 Marilyn Lloyd	47
4 Jim Cooper	24
5 Bill Boner	35
6 Bart Gordon	28
7 *Don Sundquist*	73
8 Ed Jones	36
9 Harold E. Ford	11

TEXAS

1 Jim Chapman	35
2 Charles Wilson	40
3 *Steve Bartlett*	83
4 Ralph M. Hall	66
5 John Bryant	19
6 *Joe Barton*	86
7 *Bill Archer*	90
8 *Jack Fields*	85
9 Jack Brooks	23
10 J.J. Pickle	36
11 Marvin Leath	65
12 Jim Wright	21
13 *Beau Boulter*	82
14 *Mac Sweeney*	79
15 E. "Kika" de la Garza	37
16 Ronald Coleman	23
17 Charles W. Stenholm	74
18 Mickey Leland	9
19 *Larry Combest*	82
20 Henry B. Gonzalez	16
21 *Lamar S. Smith*	85
22 *Tom DeLay*	89
23 Albert G. Bustamante	24
24 Martin Frost	25
25 Michael A. Andrews	35
26 *Richard Armey*	91

	%
27 Solomon P. Ortiz	28

UTAH

1 *James V. Hansen*	87
2 *Wayne Owens*	21
3 *Howard C Nielson*	84

VERMONT

AL *James M. Jeffords* 30

VIRGINIA

1 *Herbert H. Bateman*	66
2 *Owen G. Pickett*	30
3 *Thomas J. Bliley, Jr.*	74
4 Norman Sisisky	34
5 Dan Daniel	74
6 James R. Olin	35
7 *D. French Slaughter*	77
8 *Stan Parris*	64
9 Frederick C. Boucher	21
10 *Frank R. Wolf*	60

WASHINGTON

1 *John Miller*	60
2 Al Swift	15
3 Don Bonker	19
4 *Sid Morrison*	57
5 Thomas S. Foley	18
6 Norman D. Dicks	22
7 Mike Lowry	12
8 *Rod Chandler*	58

WEST VIRGINIA

1 Alan B. Mollohan	28
2 Harley O. Staggers, Jr.	18
3 Bob Wise	21
4 Nick J. Rahall II	19

WISCONSIN

1 Les Aspin	21
2 Robert W. Kastenmeier	12
3 *Steve Gunderson*	61
4 Gerald D. Kleczka	16
5 Jim Moody	12
6 *Thomas E. Petri*	66
7 David R. Obey	15
8 *Toby Roth*	73
9 F. James Sensenbrenner, Jr.	82

WYOMING

AL *Dick Cheney* 85

The Senate[3]

	%		%
ALABAMA		**INDIANA**	
Howell Heflin	64	*Richard G. Lugar**	59
Richard C. Shelby	43	*Dan Quayle*	64
ALASKA		**IOWA**	
Frank H. Murkowski	59	*Charles E. Grassley*	64
Ted Stevens	49	Tom Harkin	34
ARIZONA		**KANSAS**	
Dennis DeConcini*	48	*Robert Dole*	60
John McCain	66	*Nancy Landon Kassebaum*	48
ARKANSAS		**KENTUCKY**	
Dale Bumpers	27	Wendell H. Ford	37
David Pryor	34	*Mitch McConnell*	58
CALIFORNIA		**LOUISIANA**	
Alan Cranston	18	John B. Breaux	32
*Pete Wilson**	65	J. Bennett Johnston	43
COLORADO		**MAINE**	
William L. Armstrong	86	*William S. Cohen.**	45
Timothy E. Wirth	31	George J. Mitchell*	26
CONNECTICUT		**MARYLAND**	
Christopher J. Dodd	21	Barbara A. Mikulski	17
*Lowell P. Weicker, Jr**	22	Paul S. Sarbanes*	16
DELAWARE		**MASSACHUSETTS**	
Joseph R. Biden, Jr.	26	Edward M. Kennedy*	13
*William V. Roth, Jr**	66	John F. Kerry	22
FLORIDA		**MICHIGAN**	
Lawton Chiles*	40	Carl Levin	19
Bob Graham	35	Donald W. Riegle, Jr*	21
GEORGIA		**MINNESOTA**	
Wyche Fowler, Jr.	24	*Rudy Boschwitz..**	50
Sam Nunn	48	*Dave Durenberger**	38
HAWAII		**MISSISSIPPI**	
Daniel K. Inouye*	19	*Thad Cochran..*	57
Spark M. Matsunaga*	17	John C. Stennis*	43
IDAHO		**MISSOURI**	
James A. McClure	75	*John C. Danforth**	41
Steven D. Symms	86	*Christopher "Kit" Bond*	58
ILLINOIS		**MONTANA**	
Alan J. Dixon	37	Max Baucus	31
Paul Simon	15	John Melcher*	34

3. Approximately one-third of the Senate seats are up for election every even-numbered year. Those senators marked with an asterisk (*) hold seats which will expire in 1988.

%

NEBRASKA
J. James Exon* 49
*David Karnes** 68

NEVADA
*Chic Hecht** 71
Harry Reid 24

NEW HAMPSHIRE
Gordon J. Humphrey 85
Warren B. Rudman 56

NEW JERSEY
Bill Bradley ....*.......23
Frank R. Lautenberg* 19

NEW MEXICO
Jeff Bingaman* 32
Pete V. Domenici 57

NEW YORK
Alfonse M. D'Amato ....*.......49
Daniel Patrick Moynihan* 21

NORTH CAROLINA
Jesse Helms 91
Terry Sanford 19

NORTH DAKOTA
*Quentin N. Burdick** 27
Kent Conrad.......................27

OHIO
John Glenn ....*......25
Howard M. Metzenbaum* 18

OKLAHOMA
David L. Boren 54
Don Nickles 83

OREGON
Mark O. Hatfield 29
Bob Packwood 33

PENNSYLVANIA
*John Heinz** 36
Arlen Specter.......................32

RHODE ISLAND
*John H. Chafee** 27
Claiborne Pell 18

SOUTH CAROLINA
Ernest F. Hollings 43
Strom Thurmond 70

SOUTH DAKOTA
Thomas A. Daschle 17
Larry Pressler 53

%

TENNESSEE
Albert Gore, Jr....................22
Jim Sasser* 32

TEXAS
Lloyd Bentsen* 42
Phil Gramm 85

UTAH
Jake Garn........*.............77
*Orrin G. Hatch** 77

VERMONT
Patrick J. Leahy ...*.........21
*Robert T. Stafford** 28

VIRGINIA
*Paul S. Trible, Jr.** 64
John W. Warner..................64

WASHINGTON
Brock Adams...*...........16
*Daniel J. Evans** 45

WEST VIRGINIA
Robert C. Byrd* 35
John D. "Jay" Rockefeller IV ...23

WISCONSIN
Bob Kasten ....*.....64
William Proxmire* 52

WYOMING
Alan K. Simpson .*...........64
*Malcolm Wallop** 73

A CONCLUDING MESSAGE TO
BIBLE-BELIEVING CHRISTIANS

God has allowed difficult times to arise in order to know what is in our hearts, just as He did with His children of old. He is checking to see whether or not we will search out His ways and follow them when the going gets tough.

It's our "valley of decision," America. Let us choose wisely.

God allows evil men to have their way for a while in order to see what we will do. Will we blindly join them or will we have seeing eyes and hearing ears? Will we fret because of evil men? Will we allow ourselves to become envious of those who do wrong? Will we be slowly drawn into their ways without even checking to see if God's principles are being violated?

It's our "valley of decision," America. Let us choose wisely.

Jesus told Peter that the gates of hell will not prevail against His church. Will America's Christians hole up in their church buildings singing "Hold the fort, for I am coming"? Or, will we storm the gates (strongholds) of hell singing "Onward Christian Soldiers"?

It's our "valley of decision," America. Let us choose wisely.

One of God's prophets, Elijah, opposed 450 prophets of Baal and challenged God's people: "How long will you waver between two opinions? If the Lord is God, follow Him; but if Baal is God, follow him." Will America's Christians resound with Joshua's absolute commitment, "...as for me and my household, we will serve the Lord"? Will we serve Him in all areas of our lives? Or, will we continue to retreat from the political arena and let America's last best hope for God's renewed favor slip through our fingers forever?

It's our "valley of decision," America. Let us choose wisely.

A grand old hymn by James Russel Lowell says:

"Once to every man and nation
Comes the moment to decide,
In the strife of truth with falsehood,
For the good or evil side:
Some great cause, some great decision,
Off'ring each the bloom or blight,
And the choice goes by forever
'Twixt that darkness and that light."

It's our "valley of decision," America. Let us choose wisely.

— BIBLIOGRAPHY —

These books and videotapes (VHS) are available from General Birch Services Corp., 395 Concord Avenue, Belmont, MA 02178 or 2650 Mission Street, San Marino, CA 91108. Please add 10 percent ($1.00 minimum) for postage and handling. Prices and availability are subject to change without notice.

BOOKS:

A. Ralph Epperson, *The Unseen Hand: An Introduction to the Conspiratorial View of History* (Westlake Village, CA: American Media, 1985), $12.95, paperback. 100 books are condensed into a compact and highly readable introduction to the conspiracy.

Gary Allen, *None Dare Call It Conspiracy* (Seal Beach, CA, Concord Press, 1971), $2.00, paperback. An excellent book on the Insider conspiracy.

Samuel L. Blumenfeld, *Is Public Education Necessary?* (Old Greenwich, CT: Devin-Adair Company, 1981). $9.95, paperback. This book demonstrates that public education was never needed in America and how the socialist have used the public school movement.

Richard Wurmbrand, *Marx and Satan* (Westchester, IL: Crossway Books, 1986) $5.95, paperback. Written by a Lutheran pastor; especially pertinent in light of today's liberation theology.

VIDEO TAPES:

Keeping Faith With America. This is a reverent review of the Constitution and an analysis of those who seek to change it. $25.00, 49 minutes.

Who Shall Teach? The Case For Separation of School and State. Shows what must be done to rescue America from our deteriorating public education system. $25.00, 60 minutes.

An Overview of Our World. Provides an analysis of the Great Conspiracy. $25.00, 120 minutes.